Lifeline

THE WAR OF 1812 ALONG THE UPPER ST. LAWRENCE RIVER

Mike Phifer

HERITAGE BOOKS
2008

HERITAGE BOOKS
AN IMPRINT OF HERITAGE BOOKS, INC.

Books, CDs, and more—Worldwide

For our listing of thousands of titles see our website at
www.HeritageBooks.com

Published 2008 by
HERITAGE BOOKS, INC.
Publishing Division
100 Railroad Ave. #104
Westminster, Maryland 21157

Copyright © 2008 Mike Phifer

Other books by the author:
The Wolves from Niagara

All rights reserved. No part of this book may be reproduced or transmitted in any form or by any means, electronic or mechanical, including photocopying, recording or by any information storage and retrieval system without written permission from the author, except for the inclusion of brief quotations in a review.

International Standard Book Numbers
Paperbound: 978-0-7884-4681-8
Clothbound: 978-0-7884-7242-8

To my family

TABLE OF CONTENTS

PREFACE		vii
CHAPTER 1	THE SETTLEMENT OF THE UPPER COUNTRY 1783-1812	9
CHAPTER 2	THE ROAD TO WAR 1807-1812	23
CHAPTER 3	EARLY SKIRMISHES ON THE ST. LAWRENCE RIVER 1812	37
CHAPTER 4	BROCKVILLE AND OGDENSBURG 1813	49
CHAPTER 5	SACKETS HARBOR 1813	61
CHAPTER 6	THE BEGINNING OF WILKINSON'S CAMPAIGN 1813	73
CHAPTER 7	FAILURE AT CHATEAUGUAY 1813	85
CHAPTER 8	CRYSLER'S FARM 1813	91
CHAPTER 9	DISCONTENT ALONG THE UPPER ST. LAWRENCE 1814	107
CHAPTER 10	OSWEGO AND THE END OF THE WAR, 1814	121
CHAPTER 11	THE RETURN OF PEACE 1815 AND BEYOND	131
ENDNOTES		137
BIBLIOGRAPHY		159
INDEX		167

PREFACE

Being of Loyalists descent (my ancestors having serving in the King's Royal Regiment of New York and Butler's Rangers) and being born and raised in eastern Ontario not far from the Crysler's Farm battlefield (now mostly submerged), I have long been interested in the War of 1812. It was with great pleasure that I undertook researching and writing this book about this largely overlooked theatre of the war. No other region in Upper Canada was of more importance to the successful defence of the province than the Upper St. Lawrence River. Had this region been captured and successfully held by the Americans, Upper Canada would have fallen.

While supply laden bateaux moving up the Upper St. Lawrence River were vulnerable to attack from American forces, it was from New York and Vermont that much needed provisions, mostly on the hoof, crossed across the river to supply the British in Upper Canada. As the war progressed and victuals became harder to obtain, the inhabitants along the Upper St. Lawrence found themselves under martial law. This only added to the growing discontent of the settlers with the British.

In the following work I've attempted to shed some light on this important region during the war. The battles of Sackets Harbor and Oswego are also covered in the book. These fights did not take place along the Upper St. Lawrence River, but the operations were launched from Kingston.

I would like to thank the Williamsburg branch of the S.D.&G. Library, especially Beverly Richmire for tracking down numerous books for me who made this work possible.

Mike Phifer

CHAPTER 1
THE SETTLEMENT OF THE UPPER COUNTRY
1783 - 1812

"[W]e found a tract of the best land I ever saw lying at the west end of the Lake St. Francis and extending westerly nearly 20 miles above Oswagachie, then begins very broken land which continues to Cataracqui one Township extending 6 miles west from Catarocqui will be tollerable good Land . . .", commented Captain Justus Sherwood on October 14, 1783. He and a small party of the Queen's Loyal Rangers had been exploring and surveying the north bank of the Upper St. Lawrence for settlement. The American Revolution was over, and a wave of Loyalist refugees were flooding into Quebec joining the many already there living in camps at Three Rivers and at Sorel. By the end of the war there were around 7,000 Loyalists in Quebec. With everything lost during the war, these people needed a new home. The governor of Quebec, Sir Frederic Haldimand, after advisement by Sir John Johnson, commander of King's Royal Regiment of New York, decided to settle these people on the Upper St. Lawrence River from the modern Quebec/Ontario border to the Bay of Quinte. Sherwood, a frontiersman from Vermont, new good land when he saw it and reported to Haldimand's secretary that the "climate here is very mild & good, and I think the Loyalists may be the happiest people in America by settling this Country from Long Sou to Bay Quinty."[1]

Sherwood's party was not the only one Haldimand sent out to explore the wilderness for settlement. Lieutenant David Jones of Major Edward Jessup's Loyal Rangers paddled up the Ottawa River with a small party of men exploring both banks of that river.[2] Another officer of the same unit, Lieutenant Gershom French, paddled up the Ottawa to the Rideau River, then explored that river for possible settlements, eventually portaging to the Gananoque

River and following it to the St. Lawrence River.³

    As the southwestern part of the mighty St. Lawrence River that stretched from Lake Ontario to the Atlantic Ocean, the Upper St. Lawrence had seen few settlements. Of course the Mississaugas were there in their hunting camps and there had been other Indian tribes before them. A permanent settlement had been established by the Mohawks in 1755 at Akewsasne on the south side of the St. Lawrence River near the future Cornwall. These Mohawks had been living near Montreal where their descendants had migrated to in the 1660s from their ancestral homes in New York. They had made the journey north to be closer to Catholic missions as they had converted to that faith. Other Catholic Iroquois, this time Onondagas, had settled where a mission had been established in 1749 at Oswegatchie later called Ogdensburg (New York).⁴

    The first Europeans to the area were the French who had built a few military and fur trading posts. The biggest was Fort Frontenac (Kingston), while another was constructed on Chimney Island in the St. Lawrence near Oswegatchie called Fort Levis in 1759. The French also had a small shipbuilding site at Point du Baril (modern Maitland, Ontario). When the British took over, they repaired Fort Levis which they had blasted into ruins in 1760 and renamed it Fort William Augustus. During the American Revolution the British had a post at Oswegatchie where supply laden bateaux moving upriver could transfer their cargo onto ships for the journey across Lake Ontario. Carleton Island, located at the mouth of the St. Lawrence River, replaced Oswegatchie in 1778 as the transhipment point.

    The importance of the Upper St. Lawrence River for the Europeans was that it led to the heart of the continent. Indian trade goods and military supplies moved upriver and furs down river. The St. Lawrence however was not an easy river to travel on. There were rapids and this was why a transhipment post was established at Oswegatchie and later Carleton Island.

    From Montreal upriver to modern Cardinal (Ontario) there were a series of rapids that plagued shipping. The first set of rapids were at Lachine near Montreal. In 1680 a plan was developed by monks from the Sulpician Order in Montreal to bypass these roaring, churning waters with a small canal. It would be a number of years before an attempt was made and the project ran out of money in 1701 before completion. A later attempt in 1717 to resume construction failed as well.[5]

The next series of rapids on the river were at the 'Cascades', the 'Cedars' and 'Coteau' located between Lake St. Louis and Lake St. Francis. In 1779, Captain William Twiss of the Royal Engineers undertook to construct a canal and locks at Coteau-du-Lac to bypass the rapids. The canal was 900 feet long, 6 feet wide and had depth of 2 ½ feet. There were three locks in it. To protect the canal and locks, two blockhouses were constructed. There were also two warehouses built at the same time. The canal was completed in 1781 and although they were built for military use in allowing men and material to move quicker upriver, merchants were allowed to use them as well at a toll of 10 shillings per bateau.

In 1783, three more canals were dug. The first was 400 feet long and located at the Faucille Rapids and had one lock. The second was 200 feet long and no lock was needed. It was located at Trou-du-Moulin. Finally the third was constructed at Split Rock. The canal here was 200 feet long and had one lock. As with the first canal a toll was charged to merchants to use these canals although the price was higher at 25 shillings. With these military canals the rapids at Coteau and the Cascades were bypassed. Between 1801-1805 these canals were improved.

The Long Sault Rapids (near Cornwall) were next and they stretched for about nine miles. The roar of the rapids at Long Sault were described "as an object of terror and delight," by an early river traveler.[6] The next series of rapids were at the Rapid de Plat (near Morrisburg, Ontario) and the Gallops (near Cardinal).[7] This was the last rapid and shortly upriver would begin the Thousand Islands stretching to the head of the river. It was a scenic area, where the islands varied in size and shape, some were wooded, while others were not.

With the coming of the Loyalists the Upper St. Lawrence or upper country as it was referred to was about to change dramatically. Before the land could be settled, it had to be purchased from the Mississauga Indians. Johnson ordered Captain William Crawford, Indian agent at Carleton Island, to meet with Mississaugas and purchase all the land from along the north bank from the seigniory of Longueuil to the Bay of Quinte. This is now a good chunk of modern eastern Ontario. In return the Indians received clothes, a new fusil for those who did not have one already, powder and ball for the winter hunt, laced hats and enough red cloth to make a dozen coats or so. On October 9, Crawford was writing to Johnson telling him that the "Mississaugas appear much satisfied that the white people are coming to live among them."[8]

Concerned for the settlement of his men and their families, Johnson sent out surveyors to lay out townships in March of 1784. In a letter to Haldimand, Johnson proposed that the settlement of the Loyalists in his 1st Battalion of the King's Royal Regiment of New York be divided according to ethnicity and religion. This was agreed to. The first five townships from the modern Quebec/Ontario border west were Charlottenburgh to be settled by Scottish Roman Catholics, Cornwall by Scottish Presbyterians, Osnabruck by German Calvinists, Williamsburgh by German Lutherans and Matilda by Anglicans.[9] There were three more townships that were to be settled by Loyalists from Jessup's Corps or those associated with it. They were Edwardsburgh, Augusta and Elizabethtown.

The next townships were around Cataraqui and the Bay of Quinte area. There five townships were Kingston, Ernestown, Fredericksburgh, Adolphustown and Marysburgh. The first township was settled by about 200 Associated Loyalists from New York City. This band of Loyalists was led by a Captain Michael Grass who had been a prisoner a Fort Frontenac during the Seven Years War. Grass had received permission from Sir Guy Carleton, commander of British Forces in North America to do so. The rest of the townships were to be settled by the rest of Jessup's Corps, the 2nd Battalion of the King's Royal Regiment of New York, the King's Rangers, some Hessians and more Associated Loyalists from New York City under Major Peter Van Alstyne.[10] Also in the Bay of Quinte area were 100 Mohawks under John Deserontyon who had been offered land there by the British for their allegiance during the war.[11]

Besides the townships, three town sites were laid. One at New Johnston, which would be changed to Cornwall, another called New Oswegatchie later called Johnstown, (located about 5 miles down river from Prescott). Cataraqui was the third town site laid out and it was soon to be called Kingston. The area was ready for settlement.

With four or five families crowding into a 30-foot flat bottom bateau crewed by four or five men, the Loyalists set out from

Lachine in June of 1784. The bateaux had sails but they were only useful with a direct wind, otherwise the five or six man crew, plus a captain would row with oars or "set" the bateaux upriver "with long stout poles, shod with iron." Whether moving supplies or people, the bateaux generally traveled in brigades of ten or twelve boats led by a "conductor". By traveling in brigades the crews from the bateaux could help each one get through the rapids. When the rapids were reached, the passengers would disembark and walk around them. The crews meanwhile would get out of the bateaux, take a rope and often have to wade, stumbling and straining through the rushing water as they hauled the two or three ton boat through the rapids. Some crew members would stay aboard and help pole the bateau along as well and keep her off the shore. It was tough, bone weary work that was time consuming as each boat would have to be hauled through separately.[12]

The Loyalists settling in the first five townships reached Cornwall on June 20, 1784.[13] It was here they drew their lot tickets to see where they would settle. With townships drew up in equal lots each man simply drew a lot regardless of rank. This was seen as the only fair way of granting land, although not all were happy with the procedure. Sir John Johnson thought he and the other officer should get first pick of the lots before the enlisted men drew. Haldimand said no, everybody would draw equally. As it was, officers did receive more land. A field officer was to receive a 1000 acres of land, while a captain was to receive 700 acres and subaltern 500 acres. A non-commissioned officer was to receive 200 while a private would receive 100 acres. A civilian was to receive 50 acres as was each member of the Loyalist's family. There was some debate how much land should be given to black Loyalists. Haldimand thought they should get 50 acres while Johnson figured they should get the same as anybody else, but as many of the blacks were slaves, the land should go to the slave owner. Three years later an additional 200 acres was granted to the head of the Loyalist's family, provided they had made improvements on their original grant. It was decided that the children of the Loyalists when they became of age would be granted 200 acres. Due to an early promise made to another Loyalist unit, the Royal Highland Emigrants (84th Regiment), the land grants for officers was raised to 5,000 for field officers, 3,000 for captains and 2,000 for subalterns in 1788.[14]

When the lots were drawn, everybody took their turn and then those who were to receive more than one lot drew again. This meant much of the officer's land was not in one block but rather scattered over the township. They requested that their land be awarded them in one block, but Haldimand denied them. Everybody was to be treated equal.

To help the Loyalists make a home in the wilderness, the British supplied them with provisions for three years. Each Loyalists, male or female, was provided with clothes. Each family was given a hoe, an axe and spade, while a plough and cow was granted to every two families. A whip saw and crosscut saw was provided for every fourth family. Seeds for planting were also provided as well. A grist mill was established by the British along the Cataraqui River in 1782-83. Settlers from as far east as Cornwall would have to haul their grain upriver to be milled. In 1788, the trip was considerably shortened when Messrs. Coons and Shaver established a grist mill near modern Iroquois, Ontario.

Not all the Loyalists heading for their new life on the Upper St. Lawrence came from Montreal. Some set out for their new homes from Carleton Island. Once the Loyalists had drawn their lots, they then located their land and began to clear enough land to put up a small log cabin or shanty.

Well over 3,700 Loyalists had moved upriver from Lachine in 1784 and settled along the Upper St. Lawrence. The Niagara region and the area across the Detroit river from Detroit were also seeing Loyalists settlements as well. Not all was well among the Loyalist settlers along the St. Lawrence River. They began to petition the government "that the blessing of British laws and British Government and exemption from the French tenures" be extended to the new settlements.[15] The Loyalists did not like the idea of living under a seigneurial system with the crown being their seigneur. Some of the settlers, led by Patrick McNiff began to believe that the officers wanted a seigneurial system as in Quebec, which the officers in actuality did not want. They suspected their former officers wanted to keep their social status they had obtained during the war. This did not sit well with McNiff and his followers who believed themselves equal in social status with the officers. Case in point of this exclusiveness for McNiff was the letter of congratulation the former Loyalist officers sent to Carleton, now Lord Dorchester, who replaced Haldimand as governor. The Loyalist settlers were determined to keep their rights they enjoyed through the British constitution and laws. There were some heated meeting among the officers and Loyalist settlers before things simmered down. In 1788, Dorchester organized the townships on the Upper St. Lawrence and farther west into four districts named Lunenburg, Mecklenberg, Nassau and Hesse, giving them more autonomy.[16]

It was also in that year that the small town of Cataraqui had its name changed to Kingston. It was about this time that Governor Lord Dorchester was debating "whether Carleton Island or Kingston should be the more eligible station for the king's ships of war, to protect the navigation of Lake Ontario and the upper part of the River St. Lawrence."[17] Carleton Island was seen as the better choice by Deputy Surveyor General John Collins but with that island in American territory as agreed to under the peace treaty of 1783 Kingston was chosen. After the American Revolution the British decided to hold onto the western posts at Oswegatchie, Carleton Island, Niagara, Detroit and Michilimackinac which were critical to preserving a British/Indian alliance. This was an important factor in the defence of the infant colony of Upper Canada. The importance of these posts to the fur trade was not lost to the British either. Although this was in violation of the peace treaty that ended the American Revolution, the British kept the posts stating that United States was not living up to its end of the treaty by providing restitution to the Loyalists for confiscated property and preventing persecution of the Loyalists.

Known as 'the Hungry Year',1788 (some areas it lasted longer) brought hardship to the Loyalist settlements when the previous year poor harvest caused a severe food crisis. Settlers were forced to live off roots, buds and weeds. Beef bones were boiled along with some wheat bran for a weak soup. The bones were then passed on to the neighbors so they could do the same. In some cases the family pet was eaten. Despite these desperate measures some people starved to death. Lord Dorchester finally allowed importation of food from the United States duty free which helped ended the suffering. Had he done this earlier, until waiting till the end of the famine, much suffering might have been alleviated.

In 1791 Upper Canada was born. The Loyalists finally got their wish of not being apart of Quebec and the siegneurial system.

The Canada or Constitutional Act of 1791 created two colonies - Lower Canada and Upper Canada. With the formation of Upper Canada came a lieutenant governor, who ran the province in absence of the governor in Lower Canada. He was John Graves Simcoe and he quickly brought disappoint to Kingston. It was hoped Kingston would be the capital of the new colony, but Simcoe eventually decided on Newark (modern Niagara-on-the-Lake) and later settled on the small town of York (modern Toronto).

Simcoe recommended in the early 1790s as war loomed with the Americans due to tensions in the old Northwest, that as Kingston was too vulnerable to a winter attack over the ice, the naval and military establishment should be moved to York. Nothing was done. The signing of the Jay Treaty of 1794 muted any saber rattling. In the next six years the Kingston naval establishment was expanded, with naval and transport stores, a work shed and sail loft being built on Point Frederick.[18] As late as March 1812, recommendations were still made to move the naval station to York as it was believed the harbor could be easier protected. As before no move was ever made.

Under Simcoe the new colony of Upper Canada was divided into 19 counties. The four districts names were changed to the Eastern, Midland, Home and Western Districts. The population of Upper Canada skyrocketed as Simcoe open the door for American settlement. Upper Canada needed settlers and Simcoe thought Americans, who he believed that many still had some loyalty for the crown, would make good settlers as they knew how to survive and make a home in the wilderness. Thousands of Americans took him on his offer of free land (although there was a patent fee) and moved across the border. By 1812 about two-thirds of the population of Upper Canada were recent arrivals from the United States. Roughly one-sixth of the population were American Loyalists and their off spring.[19]

In 1798, because of the population boom, the district were reorganized. On the Upper St. Lawrence the Eastern district now consisted of Dundas, Stormont and Glengarry counties. Leeds and Grenville counties made up the Johnstown District. To the north was Carleton County which was attached to the Johnstown District. The Midland District of Frontenac came next after the Johnstown District and included the counties of Lennox, Addington, and Hastings and Prince Edward. Most of these last few counties were in the Bay of

Quinte area and not along the St. Lawrence. The rest of districts in the province were Newcastle, Home, Niagara, London and Western.[20]

With the population growth of Upper Canada reaching to around 77,000 by 1811, Kingston was quickly becoming the most important town in the colony, both militarily and commercially. This was due largely to its location at the head of the St. Lawrence River. The town had become the transhipment point for ships on Lake Ontario and bateaux on the river. One of the town's most prominent merchant, Richard Cartwright, was instrumental in the economical growth of the not only Kingston, but of the young colony.

Born in Albany, New York in 1759, Cartwright had served as a secretary to John Butler and his fearsome Rangers for part of the revolution. In 1780 he left Butler's Rangers and became partners with Robert Hamilton. A third partner from Detroit, John Askin, joined a year later. Besides being involved in the fur trade the men expanded their business to supply the British garrisons. By 1783, Cartwright was working out of Carleton Island. The following year the partnership with Askin ended. It was around this time that Cartwright moved his operations to Cataraqui and continue to work with Hamilton until 1790.

As the colony grew Cartwright and other merchants located in Kingston greatly prospered. Cartwright not only exported wheat, lumber, potash, flour and other products down river to his agents at Montreal, he also imported manufactured goods from England to be sent upriver to sell to the local settlers. In 1794, Cartwright and others shipped over 12,800 bushels of wheat and almost 900 barrels of flour down the St. Lawrence River. Cartwright was also a contractor supplying the British garrisons in Upper Canada (or in American territory till 1796) with salt pork. This was not all. Cartwright was involved in ship building for service on Lake Ontario as well as scows for the river to ship his flour to skirt the steep prices charged by the navigation companies in their bateaux. Besides being a merchant, Cartwright in the mid 1780s became the justice of the peace. This was only the start of his public career. He was shortly after appointed a judge of the Court of Common Pleas. Cartwright had many other appointments as well. He was a commissioner for the Midland District, a militia officer, and legislative councillor among other things.[21]

A settlement further down river that was soon to threaten Kingston in the forwarding trade was Prescott. Major Jessup's founded the town in 1810, when he had a portion of his large land grant surveyed into town lots and streets. The following year, the first house was built in Prescott by William Gilkison who was interested in getting involved in the forwarding trade. Born in Irvine, Scotland in 1777, Gilkison as a young man went to sea aboard a merchant vessel. The French captured the ship he worked on and Gilkison soon found himself imprisoned. Held for almost a year, Gilkison managed to escape. By 1796 he arrived in North America and was soon commanding one of John Jacob Astor's schooners in the employment of the North West Company on Lake Erie. By 1810 he was living in Brockville.[22]

By 1812, Jessup's little settlement consisted of three houses, one of which was built of stone. There were also two barns and two outbuildings used as a school house and store house. Besides these structures, Jessup had about 90 acres of land under cultivation, with another 60 acres of grazing land. This cleared land would have been cluttered with many stumps. Jessup had also an orchard of 400 young apple trees.[23] This little settlement would become of extreme importance during the coming war.

Settlement of the New York side of the St. Lawrence River was slower getting started than that of the Upper Canadian side. After the remaining New York Iroquois signed away much of their territory a few years after the 1783 peace treaty, the land was opened up for settlement. The land was auctioned off in 1787 and much of it was scooped up by a handful of speculators, the principal one being Alexander Macomb. In 1792, the Governor of New York in his annual message mentioned that 5,542 170 acres had been sold in less than 40 parcels. The land sale had brought in over £412 173. Macomb had applied for all the vacant land between Lake Champlain and the St. Lawrence but was rejected due to the size he wanted. He however reapplied again, this time for less amount of land but including much of northern New York and his application was accepted. The land he bought for 8 pence per acre. Macomb sent an agent to Europe to sell the land.[24]

The key town on the St. Lawrence was Ogdensburg (Oswegatchie). Settlement was opened in 1797 when the proprietor

Samuel Ogden's agent, Nathan Ford, began to sell land there. Previously however Ogden and associates who owned 10 townships of land along the St. Lawrence were having trouble with what he described as "trespasses daily committed on said townships, by subjects of the government of Great Britain." A saw mill had been set up by Verne Francis Lorimier, a half pay captain who had been in the employment of the British Indian Department. Timber was being cut down on Ogden's land and being rafted down to Montreal. The mill was located about 200 or 300 yards away from the British held Fort Oswegatchie.[25]

Ogden wrote to Simcoe requesting the trespassers be removed. Simcoe responded by saying "that last autumn on the representation of the Oswegatchie Indians, the magistrates of the town of Augusta, warned some of his majesty's inhabitants to quit those very lands." Simcoe pointed out that the treaty line was not "acknowledged by Great Britain, until the prior articles of the treaty shall be fulfilled by the United States." The lieutenant governor of Upper Canada was referring to the British decision to hold onto the western posts. Simcoe stated further: " . . . as this question does not concern his majesty's subjects, who have already been forbidden at the request of the Indians claiming the land, to form settlements on that side of the river, I can only refer you to his excellency the commander-in-chief."[26]

Ogden presented his case to Lord Dorchester in a letter stating that he had shown Lorimier his title of the land from the state of New York and "the injury that arise to me from the waste of timber which the mill would occasion, I offered in order to prevent any further difficulty, to pay him his disbursements in case he would desist." Lorimier refused stating "he was a conductor of the Indians, on whose land is was, and that so long as one of them were alive, he should possess the mill." Ogden stated it was not his business to determine the Indians right to the land, which he believed the "governor of New York had been long since purchased of them" or on "the propriety of the detention of the post of Oswegatchie."[27]

Ogden's problem was cleared up when the Jay's Treaty was signed which would finally see the British give up the posts they held on American territory and withdraw all troops by June 1, 1796, with the exception of Carleton Island were a handful of soldiers remained. Nathan Ford with a company of men headed to Oswegatchie to survey and settle the area. "On your arrival at Oswegatchie," Ogden ordered Ford, "endeavor in as amicable a manner as possible, to gain immediate possession of the works, mills and town." Ogden didn't think Ford would have trouble getting the fort, the mills might prove more difficult, but every exertion was to be made to get them.[28]

Like the settlements on the other side of the St. Lawrence River, this waterway was of extreme importance to the settlers of northern New York. Much of the trade from northern New York was with Upper Canada or Montreal. Salt and potash were major exports for the upstate settlers that were sent down river, while a lot of their goods were imported upriver from Montreal.[29]

In 1807, the threat of war hampered the growth of Ogdensburg as did other parts of northern New York. Many settlers feared the British would unleash Indian warriors against their farms. At the same time there was talk that Ogdensburg might become important in the forward trading on the St. Lawrence River, taking away business from Cartwright and the other Kingston merchants. "Two of the principal merchants residing at the head of the lake" called on Ford at Ogdensburg wanting to know if arrangements could be made for the "receiving and forwarding" of their produce to market "provided they should be able to contract with the owners of vessels, so as to make it their interest to come to Ogdensburgh, instead of Kingston." Much of this depended if the talk of war blew over. Of course there was no war in 1807, but Kingston still remained dominant in the transhipment business because of its commercial activities and its connection with the British military and naval presence there.[30] However, Ogdensburg would soon threaten again.

In 1809, David Parish arrived at Ogdensburg helping to make it a thriving village. Parish came from Germany, the son of Englishman living there. He was a banker who had come to the United States on behalf of a commercial house from Amsterdam, which had along with some other principal European merchants had an agreement with Napoleon to transfer a substantial amount of credit from the Spanish colony of Mexico to Europe. The specie was used to buy colonial produce in the United States and shipped to Europe under an American flag. Fast ships with hand-picked crews were used to run the blockade the Royal Navy was setting up against French controlled ports. These same ships brought the funds back to

America. The enterprise was very successful and proved lucrative to those involved.

It was while in Philadelphia engaged in this enterprise that Parish came in contact with financial men who were involved with land purchases and settlement of northern New York. Parish soon got involved, sending his land agent Joseph Rosseel to make a report of the country. Parish ended up buying a large tract of land in the area including much of Ogdensburg, that was not already sold. Parish soon undertook improving his vast property. In 1810, a large stone store was built in Ogdensburg, a large home and a couple of schooners.[31]

Parish attempted to challenge the Kingston's monopoly on the forward trade, apparently by forming a partnership of sorts with William Gilkison at Prescott. Another of the Parish's agents Silivus Hoard wrote to his employer on July 5, 1811 of their rivals at Kingston:

"I am very well informed of the Kingstonians looking still with envy upon this & more particularly upon Mr. Gilkerson's [Gilkison's] Establishment at Prescott, that they entertain hopes of bringing the traffic back into their Channel once more, and that they will next year make a strenuous effort to effect this purpose. As under the present circumstances the Interest not only of the commerce but also that of every Individual of Kingston is considerably hurt. They will, of course, form a League & be on the watch to defeat the rival Establishments."[32]

Hoard was right on the league being formed at Kingston. Rosseel wrote to Parish twenty days later stating "We are in a measure shut out of the Shipping Places on the Lake Ontario; because we are unable to bear up in competition with the whole Body of Lake Traders leagued together for the purpose of excluding us . . ."[33] The following year, as even a state of war now existed, competition for the forwarding trade still continued. Rosseel was writing in late July 1812 that "several of the houses in Kingston" were "laying a Collosal plan, by which to attract the forwarding business once more to that place." They were charging 3 cents "on a barrel of Flour, & other articles in proportion, lower than the charges we have just published." Rosseel continued, "Mr. Gilkerson

[Gilkison] appears much allarmed at the Kingston Stir. He intends to ensure all the produce, ashes excepted, which will go down through his hands at 5 p cent premium on the prime costs."[34]

As the war progressed Kingston would retain its importance in the forwarding trade. Interestingly Ogdensburg would be important too, not in the forwarding trade as this was now largely moving provisions, military and naval supplies now, but in supplying the British forces in Upper Canada.

CHAPTER 2
THE ROAD TO WAR
1807-1812

While Upper Canada and northern New York's population grew, war clouds were hovering on the horizon. Great Britain was at war with Napoleonic France in 1793 and except for brief recesses of peace, would be so until 1815. As Napoleon expanded his empire across Europe and attempted to assert his power in other places such as Egypt, the British tried to thwart him and protect their island. Much of the protection was done by the Royal Navy, although by 1809, Britain had an army in the Iberian Peninsula under Sir Arthur Wellesley (later the Duke of Wellington).

On the western frontier another Indian war was brewing. The Shawnee leader Tecumseh and his brother Tenskwatawa were attempting to build an Indian confederacy to present a common front against American expansionism. Kentuckians and other westerns believed the British Indian Department at Amherstburg were stirring up and arming the Indians. There was an element of truth to their suspicions. As war seemed imminent with the United States, the British began renewing their relations with the old northwest Indians, which had deteriorated after a serious Indian defeat at the battle of Fallen Timbers in 1794. The British Indian agents tried to make it clear to the various northwest tribes that they would not receive any assistance from the British until war actually broke out. "My tomahawk is now up but do not strike until I give the signal," said Indian Department officer Matthew Elliot to the Sac and Fox tribes.[35] The British Indian Department was under orders not to hand out powder and lead to tribes anxious to go to war, but at the same time the British wanted to keep them ready.[36] The dreams of the Indian confederacy were destroyed when the Governor of Indiana, William Henry Harrison led a force of 900 regulars and militia in early

November, 1811 against Tenskwatawa's village, Prophetstown, along the Tippecanoe Creek. The Indians were defeated and the village destroyed. Tecumseh who was absent at the time of the battle, returned to lead his warriors to Amherstburg. Many in the western states believed that only after the British were driven out of Canada would their frontier be safe.

It was at sea that brought much of the tension between Great Britain and the new United States. As a neutral power in war with Napoleon, the Americans were doing a brisk business at sea in exporting and freighting goods. Britain took a dim view of the rapidly growing American shipping industry which was cutting into their business especially after they had swept the French merchant fleet (and naval fleet) from the oceans. The situation intensified when in 1806, the British set up a blockade of France from Elbe to Brest. Napoleon responded with the order to seize ships if they stopped at a British port or were carrying goods originating from Great Britain. In turn, the Britain ordered a blockade of all ports not allowing British vessels to enter. Exception were made, but these ships would have to stop in England first and pay a steep duty. Napoleon reacted by having any ship seized after entering one of his controlled ports if they had payed this duty or submitted to search by the Royal Navy.[37]

The Americans who were having their maritime rights trampled upon, also had the indignity of having their ships stopped by the Royal Navy to search for deserters. With the expansion of American maritime trade early in the war and the release of thousands of British sailors during a brief peace with Napoleon, many of these men took work on American ships. Here they found better pay and better conditions then they did in the Royal Navy. The Royal Navy on the other hand, with the renewal of war needed men again. To get them they stopped American ships and seized anyone they thought was British. Often American sailors would be pressed into Royal Navy service even though by 1796 many of them carried certificates identifying them as American citizens.[38]

In 1807, the H.M.S. *Leopard* demanded the U.S.S. *Chesapeake* allow a boarding party to search the American ship for deserters. The commander of the *Chesapeake* refused. The *Leopard* let loose three broadsides into the American ship, killing 3 men and wounding 18 more. A Royal Navy boarding party then climbed aboard the *Chesapeake* and seized four men they determined were deserters. It was later determined only one of the men seized was a British citizen who was hung, while the others were eventually returned with an offer by the British to pay reparation.[39]

The relationship between Great Britain and the United States, which was already deteriorating, now took a turn for the worse with this incident. The American government in response to the blockade and mistreatment of their maritime rights, imposed an embargo late in 1807 which prohibited goods and ships from leaving the United States. Instead of forcing Britain and France to lift their sanctions, the embargo seriously hurt the American economy. In 1809 the embargo act was replaced by non-intercourse act, which restricted trade with Britain and France, but opened it elsewhere. However the results were the same as the embargo - devastating.[40]

The embargo hit northern New York hard which depended on trade with Montreal and Upper Canada. Oswego, along Lake Ontario, which shipped mostly salt had a trade worth almost $1,000,000 a year. Now with the embargo this trade was cut off. The settlers in northern New York if they wanted to survive began smuggling. With potash selling at around $300 a ton because of the embargo in Montreal it was worth the risk. Roads were built leading to St. Lawrence River to smuggle the goods out. Captain Jacob Brown of the 108th Regiment of the New York militia and leading settler in the area, built a road from the Black River to the St. Lawrence. Augustus Sacket, the custom collectors for the St. Lawrence region and founder of Sackets Harbor, located along Lake Ontario on the south side of Black River Bay where much of the potash was shipped out of, resigned his position instead of enforcing the embargo.

Troops were sent into the area to prevent smuggling, but soon found the local population resented their presence. The new custom collector at Sackets Harbor, Hart Massey, was threatened with death on a regular basis. Besides Sackets Harbor, troops were sent to Oswego where a sixteen gun brig called the *Oneida* was constructed to help enforce the embargo. Troops were posted at Ogdensburg in 1809, but they were unpopular with local residents. Hart Massey wrote in 1809 that the residents of Ogdensburg had threatened that if he "or any other officer should come there again, they will take a rawhide to them, which they declare they have prepared for that purpose." Massey was unmoved by the threats. The soldiers and militia were not popular as Massey added that the "people in the vicinity of their station are hostile, and refuse to accommodate them with anything, even to admit them to their houses." The citizens of Ogdensburg were glad to see them go when they eventually left town.[41] Soldiers were also to be sent to Carleton Island, where smugglers were operating out of. There was a problem though. A handful of British troops were stationed there.

Augustus Sacket on August 19, 1808, wrote to Richard Cartwright asking him to pass the letter onto the proper authorities informing them that United States troops were to be sent to Carleton Island. Sacket asked that British troops stationed there be removed. Major H. MacKenzie, commander at Kingston, visited Carleton Island and was informed that it was rumored that two armed boats were to arrive at the island to prevent smuggling. Mackenzie reinforced the four man garrison on the island with another six men.

On August 22, Lieutenant Cross of the U.S. Artillery stationed at Sackets Harbor wrote to Mackenzie reminding him that Carleton Island was in U.S. territory and asked who he should address about having the British troops removed. Mackenzie replied that he was going to keep possession of the island. He did suggest Cross have his government address Sir James Craig, Captain-General and Governor-in-Chief of British North America. Mackenzie sent a copy of the letter to Craig and to the Lieutenant-Governor of Upper Canada, Francis Gore.[42]

Craig's orders were for Carleton Island to be held, but if the American attempted to take it, the garrison was to let them have it. The situation would then be negotiated between the governments should such an occurrence take place.[43] War tension was high, especially after the *Chesapeake* affair, and no one wanted to be the spark that set off a war. The presence of U.S. troops on the border did not go unnoticed however and did create some alarm on the Upper Canadian side of the river.

Richard Cartwright was reporting on November 2, 1808 to Mackenzie from his informants that 200 U.S. regular troops "have been stationed between Great Sodus, about 20 miles to the Westward of Oswego and Ogdensburg . . . .." More troops were said to be on the march to Ogdensburg, bringing to the number up to a 1,000 men. The number was to increase to 2,000 before spring. Also causing alarm was the 18 gun vessel being constructed in Ogdensburg. The vessel was to have a 24-pounder on her bow. Cartwright was also suspicious of two American naval officers who were aboard a schooner which was driven into Kingston under the pretense of weather. He thought the officers were there "for the express purpose of examining the different Entrances" to the port of Kingston.[44]

Three days later Cartwright was writing to Gore about an incident involving Hart Massey "seizing a Boat belonging to one of His Majesty's Subjects" in waters "we have always considered as the Limits of this Province" on October 31. The boat, Cartwright admitted, had been regularly involved in the smuggling trade all summer by landing on the New York shore "and clandestinely carrying away Pot Ash and other articles in contravention of their Embargo." When captured, the boat was headed to Wolfe Island to take on potash smuggled there from Sackets Harbor.

An American boat with a crew of eight men carrying potash near the southeastern shore of Wolfe Island was being pursued by Massey, a colonel, a Lieutenant Bebie and a party of soldiers in the revenue cutter. The smugglers ran their boat up on the shore of Wolfe Island where Massy seized the boat and its cargo. Another boat, this one belonging the Andrew Denyke from Kingston and the one Cartwright referred to, was proceeding about 30 yards from the southeastern shore of Wolfe Island. Massey sent Bebie to investigate the boat. Denyke would later say the Lieutenant found nothing and returned to Massey. Denyke meanwhile continued on but not for long. Fifteen minutes later as he was passing the revenue cutter and her prize, Denyke was ordered by Massey to round to. Denyke refused to stop this time. Massey ordered him and his crew "to come along-side or they were all dead men". The soldiers took up their muskets at Massey's order but held their fire. Denyke quickly headed for Wolfe Island running his boat on shore. Then Denyke yelled back a Massey "that he was when in the King's Territory and that they had no right to meddle with him." Massey shouted back he would risk it and took possession of Denyke's boat with a party of soldiers. Massey then informed Denyke that he and his men could take their personal belongs and be landed anywhere they pleased but that Massey was keeping the boat. Denyke replied he was not quitting his boat. Massey then ordered Denyke and three others to take the boat to his deputy. The men would be paid for their time and expenses.

Not being able to find Massey's deputy, the men landed the boat three miles down river on the New York side at the home of Captain Hubbard where they planned to have supper. One man was left in the boat, while Denyke and the others were preparing supper. It was at this time Denyke saw his chance to escape and did so. Getting into his boat and cutting the cable, Denyke escaped taking with him the guard who had fallen asleep aboard the boat. In his haste to escape, Denyke left his son behind who had accompanied him.[45]

A similar event happened on June 4, 1812 when three Canadian schooners were spotted by the captain of the *Oneida*, Lieutenant Melanchton Woolsey, who believed them to be heading to the Genesee River. The *Oneida* set out in pursuit and managed to over take one of the schooners, the *Lord Nelson* recently out of Prescott, late the following day. The captain of the schooner told Woolsey that he was destined for Newark, when pressed however, he was unable to produce the proper clearance papers from American authorities. The vessel was seized and taken to Sackets Harbor where her cargo was auctioned off. The other schooners meanwhile managed to escape.[46] This was one of the last instances of peaceful confrontation as war lay only a couple of weeks away.

Ironically, as the American congress debated declaring war, the Royal Navy was under orders to avoid any trouble with the U.S. Navy and show restraint in dealing with American merchants. Great Britain offered the American merchants a fair share in the trade with Europe if they would do so under British licenses. The American government declined the offer as they saw this as giving up their sovereignty. The British in their attempts to make conciliatory efforts to the Americans dropped the blockade and the issuing of licenses. It was too late as the British foreign secretary was making the announcement to drop the blockade, the American were voting on declaring war.[47]

The House of Representatives voted in favor of war 79 to 49 on June 4, 1812. Thirteen days later the Senate passed the bill with a much closer vote of 19 in favor and 13 opposed. The country was divided over the war. Much of the northeast was against the war, while the western and southern states were in favor of war. Most of the War Hawks came out of these states. These were mostly anti-British young politicians who were determined that the only way to rectify the United States's grievance was militarily. Most of New

York's representatives voted against the war. St. Lawrence County, where Ogdensburg was located, was largely opposed to the war, probably largely due to their trade with the Canadas.

The War Hawks may have wanted war, but their country was ill prepared for one. In the months before war was declared, the government had attempted to boost the strength of the army from around 4,000 men to over 35,000. By May, the army numbered over 6,700 men.[48] Despite this, many Americans viewed the conquest of Upper Canada as a simple undertaking. With the bulk of the population in Upper Canada being from the United States it was believed by many that American troops would be welcomed as liberators. Thomas Jefferson summed up their feelings when he commented in 1812, "The acquisition of Canada this year as far as the neighbourhood of Quebec will be a mere matter of marching."[49]

"The Militia from the bay of Quinte to Glengary is the most respectable of any in the Province," wrote Major-General Isaac Brock, commander of the forces in Upper Canada to Lieutenant General Sir George Prevost, the Governor General of the Canadas and commander-in-chief of British North America who replaced Craig. Brock's predecessor, Gore, had a similar opinion when he wrote to then Governor Craig in Lower Canada that generally "the inhabitants from Kingston to the borders of the lower province may be depended upon." Other parts of the province's loyalty was more questionable due to the large immigration from the United States. Not everyone's loyalty in eastern Upper Canada was assured either. In 1811 the principal inhabitants from that portion of the province sent an address to the Lieutenant Governor informing him that they could not conceal from him "that the sudden and indiscriminate influx of foreigners, sometimes openly, and at other times secretly hostile to the British Government . . . ."[50]

Major General Isaac Brock who besides commanding the troops in Upper Canada, became the president of the Council and administrator in 1811 when Gore left for England to see to personal matters. Now at war with the United States, Brock had a real challenge to defend Upper Canada. Prevost, who directed the war and who's prime responsibility was the defence of British North American, was cautious and preferred a defensive strategy for most of the conflict. The Governor General preferred "to avoid committing any act which may even by a strained construction tend to unite the Eastern and Southern States." This did not mean he was against any offensive action, but only if the British were "to derive an immediate, considerable, and important advantage."[51] If Upper Canada was lost, it could be recaptured when fresh troops from across the Atlantic Ocean became available, but Quebec City in Prevost's war strategy had to be held no matter what. With this in mind, he kept the bulk of the regular troops - about 4,000- in Lower Canada, while Brock had only 1,200 regulars to protect the long frontier of Upper Canada.

Besides his regulars, Brock had Indian support, mostly from the western and Great Lake tribes, which he had urged the Indian Department and fur traders to garner. Brock also had the Provincial Marine, managed by the quartermaster general, which freighted men and supplies for the military. At the start of war the Provincial Marine, under the command of Master and Commander Hugh Earl, had two ships operating on Lake Ontario, the biggest being the *Royal George*. There was a third ship that was out of service and served as a hospital and winter barracks anchored at Point Frederick. Also operating out of Kingston were two Provincial Marine schooners.[52]

Fencible units were raised in the colonies of British North America. These regiments were well trained and disciplined and liable to serve anywhere in North America. In Upper Canada, the fencible regiment formed was the Glengarry Light Infantry. Initially a proposal was made to form a regiment raised from Glengarry County in 1806 and again in early 1807. Lack of support in getting men to enlist in the Canadian Fencibles dampened any idea of attempting to form another unit and the plan was put on hold. In late 1811 the plan was reintroduced to the War Office. Both Brock and Prevost endorsed the plan in early 1812, which was accepted by the War Office with some modifications. Recruitment for the regiment was expanded to both Canadas, as well as Nova Scotia and Prince Edward Island. Recruiting in 1812 was greatly helped by Captain George 'Red' Macdonell from the 8th Regiment of Foot. Given the rank of major, Macdonell with the help of Reverend Alexander Macdonell set out to enlist men into the regiment in the Canadas and especially from Glengarry County were they had clan ties. Other recruiting officers were sent out to recruit in various districts of the four colonies. In the end most men who joined the Glengarry Light

Infantry did not come from Glengarry County and most were not Scottish.[53] Command of the Glengarries was not given to Macdonell who was only to lead the unit if it did not reach full strength. Recruitment went well and command was given to Colonel Edward Baynes, Prevost's adjutant-general. Lieutenant Colonel Francis Battersby was second in command.[54]

The militia in Upper Canada was thought to be able to field about 11,650 men. There were problems though. Brock was dismayed by the lack of loyalty in the province especially among the legislators, magistrates and militia officers who believed the province would fall. On July 29, 1812, Brock was writing to Adjutant-General Colonel Edward Baynes: "My situation is most critical, not from any thing the enemy can do, but from the disposition of the people - The population, believe me is essentially bad - A full belief possess them all that this Province must inevitably succumb." Four years earlier, Gore had wrote to the Governor in Quebec that the militia would not serve if they thought the province was going to be abandoned by the British. Gore went onto say, "There are few people here that would act with Energy, were it not for the purpose of defending the lands they actually possess."[55] In western Upper Canada the militia refused to march against the American force under Brigadier General William Hull at Detroit. The situation was not much better elsewhere in the province. In the Niagara region for example, Brock had to let half his militia return to work on their farms. "Most of the people have lost all confidence - I however speak loud and look big."[56] Many Upper Canadians simply wanted to stay out of the coming war. Cartwright noted 13 years earlier that many of the people in his area that recently moved from the United States did not have any preference for the British government, however he stated he was not "inclined to impute to such of them as emigrate to this Province either hostile or treacherous views." They had probably come just to acquire "lands upon easy terms."[57]

The training of the militia was not the best. In 1788, Lord Dorchester ordered all men between 16 to 50 to serve in the militia. Five years later, Simcoe passed an Act for "the better regulation of the militia". Males between the ages of 16 to 60, were enrolled in the sedentary militia. In 1808, the Acts regarding the militia were altered. The militia was divided into regiments, further divided between 8 and 10 companies, each consisting of between 20 to 50 privates. Each company was to be inspected twice a year. Besides the annual muster day, where each militiaman had to present himself or face a fine of two dollars, it insisted that each man provide himself with a serviceable musket, fusil or rifle within six months of enrollment. The company captains were not to call out their men more than four times a year, but not less than two for training. Exempt from militia duty were Quakers, Mennonites and Tunkers who were required to pay 20 shillings annually in peacetime instead. In time of war the price was raised to £5.[58]

With war imminent with the United States additions were added in regards to the militia in an act that passed in March 1812. Two flank companies numbering not more than 100 men each were to be raised from each militia regiment, but not to compose more than one third of the strength of the battalion (regiment). The flank companies were composed of men under 40 who volunteered or were chosen by ballot if there were not enough volunteers. The flank companies were to train six days every month until "found duly instructed". Anybody serving in the flank companies were exempt from "any personal Arrest on any civil Process, or to serve as Juror, or to perform duty as a Town or Parish Officer, or Statute labour on the Highways, ..."[59]

Besides the flank companies, at the start of the war there was also a volunteer corps raised. In the Johnston District that would include an artillery company, a troop of cavalry and three rifle companies. Some militiamen may have served on gunboats on St. Lawrence River as well.

Adjutant General Colonel Baynes ordered on July 10, 1812 the Inspecting Field Officer of the Militia Colonel Robert Lethbridge of the 60th to inspect the militia from Cornwall to Kingston to determine their competence and to see how well they were armed and equipped. He was then to take command at Kingston and take charge of the Upper St. Lawrence. Lethbridge was under orders not to provoke the Americans, but to maintain the peace along the Upper St. Lawrence River. If the enemy made a serious attack, then Lethbridge was to make sure the military stores did not fall into the American hands and retreat to Lower Canada or join Brock further west, abandoning, at least temporarily, the Upper St. Lawrence River.

Lethbridge found the militia on the Upper St. Lawrence to

be enthusiastic, but poorly drilled and "almost in the infancy of discipline." The serving flank companies he discovered had little in the way of camp equipment. In fact many soldiers had no blankets and were using straw instead. This is not surprising as at this stage in the war as most things were in short supply. Besides blankets, there was not enough uniforms for the militia, medical supplies and even such things as lead pencils and sealing wax. Muskets were in short supply, although before setting out on his assignment, Lethbridge did learn that 200 muskets, as well as accouterment for 25 cavalrymen had been already shipped to Prescott, while a 100 were sent to Cornwall. Another 60 had been shipped to Dundas County, while 144 muskets at Cornwall were sent to Montreal for repair. Fifty ball cartridges had been supplied with each musket.[60]

At Kingston, Major Donald MacPherson agreed with Lethbridge's finding of the zeal of the militia when he commented on July 5: "I never saw men come forward with more cheerfulness or more willing to be instructed than the Militia of this and neighboring districts."

Of upmost importance to the defence of Upper Canada was holding Kingston, the main supply depot for the British army in the colony. Just as important was keeping the St. Lawrence River open to movement of supplies and personnel. William "Tiger' Dunlop a surgeon with the 89th Regiment of Foot who was stationed at Prescott for part of the war wrote of this precarious lifeline:

". . . every kind of Military and Naval Stores, every bolt of canvas, every rope yarn, as well as the heavier articles of guns, shot, cables, anchors, and all the numerous etceteras for furnishing a large squadron, arming forts, supplying arms for the militia and the line, had to be brought from Montreal to Kingston, a distance of nearly 200 miles, by land in winter, and in summer by flat-bottomed boats, which had to tow up the rapids, and sail up the parts of the river, (in many places not a mile in breadth, between the British and American shores,) exposed to the shot of the enemy without any protection."[61]

If the Americans seized control of the river, they could shut off Upper Canada's lifeline. The river had to be controlled if Upper Canada was to have a chance a survival. There was a rough road that ran from Montreal to Kingston, more suitable for traveling on horseback than wagons. At best the road could be used in the summer or in the winter, but in the spring or fall it would be a muddy quagmire. There was no way that the amount of supplies the British would need to defend Upper Canada could be moved on the road.

Although river traffic was far superior and more dependable than the road, it was expensive. It cost roughly 54 shillings a hundred weight to freight goods upriver. To move six 32-pounders for the Royal Navy to Kingston cost £2,000. Traveling in brigades of bateaux, it took about two weeks to get from Montreal to Kingston. Of course adding to the expense and time most of the military supplies had to be shipped from England to Quebec City or Sorel. From there they were taken aboard John Molson's steamboat or by bateaux to Montreal. Once they reached Kingston they then had to be shipped onto York or Fort George or wherever it was destined. It was a tenuous supply route.[62]

On April 24, 1812, the Adjutant Generals' Office declared that from May 1st "all Batteaux and other Craft of Burthen for the conveyance of Troops or the Transport of Stores, throughout the Canadas, shall be transferred to, and remain in charge of the Commissariat, ..."[63] By October 1st, the movement of goods and men upriver was run by the Corps of Canadian Voyageurs under the command of North West Company partner, William McGillivray. Accompanying the bateaux on escort duty were detachment of soldiers. On September 22 for example, Captain Pentz with a subaltern, two sergeants and 50 Canadian Fencibles were "to take with them 60 Rounds Ball Cartridge per Man, and are to be kept in separate Divisions in light Boats, in readiness to use their Arms, at a Moments Notice are not to be employed in rowing."[64]

One of the main roles of the militia on the Upper St. Lawrence was watching the river for American activity. They were also to offer protection for supply laden bateaux moving upriver. The militia could also be moved quickly east to Lower Canada should the Americans make an attempt along the Lake Champlain and Richelieu River route to attack Montreal.

To protect the river and the Upper Canadian side of the St. Lawrence, forts or fortified houses began to be built. At Prescott the militia took it upon themselves to fortify their key position along the river. When Colonel William Fraser, commander of the Grenville Militia, called out his men, he housed them in the two-storey stone house and a timber building. By July, Fraser was having a stockade of green unseasoned timber, built around the two buildings on a light rise. For three months, 15 carpenters, 36 labourers and 48 teamsters with 90 horses and oxen undertook to build the stockade. When it was completed in October, the stockade measuring 200 feet by 150 feet which had only three walls as a ravine ran along the east side which was left open. At the southeast, southwest and northwest corners there were bastions built. An earthern battery was built south east of the stockade which housed a pair of 9 pounder cannons.[65]

At Cornwall flank companies were posted in the town under the command of Lieutenant Colonel Neil McLean of the 1st Regiment of Stormont Militia. Troops were housed in the courthouse and gaol. A magazine for artillery stores and a hospital were also established in town. A guard was also posted at Glengarry Point, located along the St. Lawrence River. Another guard was also sent to watch the river from the farm of Captain Joseph Anderson of the 1st Stormont Regiment. Across the river at Massena Point an American militia guard was also posted and the two sides amused themselves by firing back and forth. The fun came to end when one of the American soldiers was wounded. There were no more shots traded back and forth.[66]

On the New York side of the river, the militia was mobilizing there as well. In April of 1812 the New York militia was divided into two divisions and eight brigades. Although the militia in the United States numbered 700,000, Congress called up 100,000 men as war grew closer. New York's quota was 13,500 detached militia, although it's state militia numbered over 100,000 men. Detached militia were better trained than the regular militia. Like their neighbors across the St. Lawrence River, the New York militia was short of supplies and equipment.

In command of the 5th Brigade was newly promoted Brigadier General Jacob Brown. In charge of defending the northern New York frontier, Brown quickly ordered the militia to be assembled and take up key position at Ogdensburg, Cape Vincent and Sackets Harbor. Men were posted in other places as well, but with only 600 militia men, troops were spread thin. Like the Upper Canadian militia, Brown had problems finding enough supplies for his men. It would not be until July 30 that a company of regular troops would arrive at Sackets Harbor to bolster the various militia regiments. Captain Benjamin Forsyth commanded the 150 men of the Regiment of Riflemen. They would prove to be excellent and aggressive soldiers. In overall charge of the northern frontier for the Americans was Major General Henry Dearborn, a veteran of the Revolutionary War. The Secretary of War was William Eustis.[67]

At the start of the war, American presence on Lake Ontario consisted of only one brig, the *Oneida,* launched at Oswego in 1809 to enforce the embargo. Lieutenant Melancthon Taylor Woolsey who commanded the brig, wasted no time in ordering the conversion of the captured *Lord Nelson* into a gunboat. Another schooner, the *Julia* was to be converted as well. At Ogdensburg there were six schooners which were greatly needed to boost the naval strength, but getting them up the St. Lawrence past the British might prove risky since they were unarmed.

Supplying the troops on the northern frontier was not only difficult, but highly expensive. Roads, like in Upper Canada, were not the best. One of the supply routes, which had seen active use during the French and Indian War and the American Revolution was along the Mohawk River, Wood Creek, the portage to Oneida Lake and onto the Oswego River, where another portage was necessary to get around the falls and then finally onto Lake Ontario. Like the St. Lawrence River, it was expensive to move supplies along this route. In 1814 for example, it cost about $1,000 to get one big gun to the American navy on Lake Ontario.

By July, Brown was headed north to the border to calm the fears of the local settlers, who feared Indians would soon begin raiding their settlements. At St. Regis (Akwesasne), located on the border along the St. Lawrence River, the Mohawks were in a precarious situation. Both sides outwardly declared that St. Regis should remain neutral, which many of the Indians themselves wanted. The American settlers however were suspicious of what side the Mohawks backed, and became alarmed each time the Indians left the reservation to hunt or fish. The settlers made the Indians carry passes if they wanted to leave their land. Eventually the U.S. government stepped in and provided 500 rations daily to the Mohawks at St. Regis. Caught between two belligerent neighbors, war would come to the reservation and divide the community.[68]

CHAPTER 3
EARLY SKIRMISHES ON THE ST. LAWRENCE RIVER
1812

With the declaration of war, Carleton Island was finally seized by the Americans, however the action was not sanctioned by Brown. Abner Hubbard, an old revolutionary veteran who ran an inn at Millens Bay, with a man and a boy decided to take matters into their own hands. Pushing off from Cape Vincent, Hubbard landed on Carleton Island to find a small four man garrison at the old British fort there. He took the soldiers and two women who lived with them prisoner and left. The prisoners were sent to Sackets Harbor. Another party returned to Carleton Island the following day and torched the buildings there.[69]

Another peaceful confrontation happened near Cornwall in early July when the British seized boats belonging to American civilians. This action alarmed the residents around Prescott, including militia officers. A letter was sent to Cornwall stating that the American commander at Ogdensburg had shown a "pacific Disposition" in regards to respecting private property. Dr. Solomon Jones, a Loyalist veteran, was sent to Cornwall to seek their release.[70] Relations between Ogdensburg and Prescott were good and possibly the residents around Prescott feared a retaliatory action by the Americans.

It was not longer after this that on July 19 a brief exchange of fire occurred between the ships of the Provincial Marine which had set out from Kingston and the American defenders at Sackets Harbor and the *Oneida*. Little damage was done to either side and the Provincial Marine soon sailed away.

At Ogdensburg a U.S. revenue cutter attempted to intercept 13 British bateaux loaded with cannon balls and ammunition heading upriver. The cutter was unable to catch the bateaux because of lack of wind and returned to town. A long boat shortly after this failed venture arrived in Ogdensburg. Aboard was Captain Noon who had orders to arrange barracks and a hospital for 1,000 troops. Also on the longboat were Oswego merchants and armed men who had come to get the trapped schooners upriver and out onto Lake Ontario where they could be taken to safety at Sackets Harbor. There had been talk about scuttling the schooners to keep them out of British hands, but this was decided against. On June 29, five of the schooners attempted to make it up river. They wouldn't get far.

On the Upper Canadian side of the river near Maitland, Dunham Jones spotted the five schooners and quickly determined the value these vessels would be to the American naval presence on Lake Ontario. He decided to stop them. Organizing a company of volunteers, Jones and his men set out after the schooners in boats. He caught up with them at the foot of the Thousands Island near Brockville. Jones and his men managed to capture two of the schooners, the *Sophia* and the *Island Packet*. The crews were landed on an island and their vessels were set a blaze. The surviving schooners turned around and retreated back to Ogdensburg, bringing word with them that Indians and whites had captured and set fire to two of the vessels. Word of an Indian attack spread along the border like wildfire. Panic gripped the border as described by Parish's agent, Joseph Rosseel: "In less than an hour all the settlements on Black Lake and St. Lawrence, from hence upwards, were entirely deserted - people every where running through the woods in great dismay."[71]

No attack or raid followed the burning of the two schooners. Tensions did not ease in Ogdensburg when a few days later the *Prince Regent* sailed down from Kingston and anchored at Prescott. Nothing happened. So far no attempt was made on the remaining schooners bottled up in Ogdensburg. For extra security the vessels were taken up the Oswegatchie River, past the bridge that led across the river to where the old French Fort Presentation lay.

Two more Provincial Marine vessels, the *Earl of Moria* and the *Duke of Gloucester*, anchored at Prescott not long afterwards. The militia stationed at Ogdensburg decided to take action against one of the vessels. Colonels T. B. Benedict and Solomon Van Rensselaer with possibly 60 volunteers planned to split into three parties and slip across the river at night in an attempt to destroy the *Duke of Gloucester*. The raid was canceled when the targeted vessel changed position.

Despite the setbacks of getting the schooners out of Ogdensburg, Brown had not given up on the idea. On July 30, he dispatched the schooner *Julia* armed with a 32-pounder and two 6-pounders under the command of Lieutenant H. W. Wells to provide escort for the trapped vessels. Supporting Wells was a rifle company under the command of Captain Noadiah Hubbard in a Durham boat. These type of boats were flat bottomed, which had a keel and centre board. They were generally anywhere from 50 to 90 feet long and had carry capacity around 40 tons. They could either be rowed, poled or sailed depending on the situation.

With only three guns and a company of riflemen, the two American vessels would have their hands full against the combined 10 carronades[72] and 10 long guns of the *Earl of Moria* and the *Duke of Gloucester*. Before departing Woolsey explained the mission to the crew and then Brown made the offer for anyone to back out of the operation if they wanted. Not one of the 60 man crew of the *Julia* did. Wells then led his tiny armada out.

The *Julia* and the Durham boat managed to slip past the *Royal George* hovering at the head of the St. Lawrence River. Around 3 P.M. on the July 31 Wells came in contact with the *Earl of Moria* and the *Duke of Gloucester* at Brockville (formerly called Elizabethtown). The *Earl of Moria* let loose with three of her carronades which did no damage to the *Julia*. Wells quickly headed for the American side of the river.

Once he got to the New York side of the river, Wells quickly brought his long guns into action. The *Earl of Moria* mostly armed with carronades was at a disadvantage as her guns didn't have the range the guns on the *Julia* did. Both sides boomed away at each other from their respective sides of the river for over three hours. The *Julia* was hit once, while the *Earl of Moria* took a few shots in her hull eventually forcing her and the *Duke of Gloucester* to have to be towed upriver by smaller boats to Brockville. There the guns of the *Earl of Moria* were taken out and placed in a battery to continue the fight. Darkness however ended the clash.

Wells had the *Julia* weigh in her anchors and continue down river to Ogdensburg. To help her along, the *Julia* was towed by her yawl boat and the Durham boat. Before morning they had reached Ogdensburg. Their mission to get the trapped schooners out of

Ogdensburg was a failure as now they were trapped in the river town as well. It would not be until early September when help would come from an unlikely source - Sir George Prevost.

In August, a ship arrived at Quebec City with word that the British had repealed the Orders in Council, one of the causes of the war. Prevost sent a messenger to Dearborn informing him of this latest development and suggested a cease fire in hopes a peace negotiation could begin with the American government. Dearborn readily agreed as it would allow him to move troops and supplies without fear of any British attacks. Before the peace attempt was rejected and hostilities resumed, the schooners from Ogdensburg were able to safely head upriver and sail to Sackets Harbor where they were converted into gunboats.

Word soon reached Ogdensburg that a brigade of bateaux was heading upriver. Not wanting to miss an opportunity on such an inviting target a small force was outfitted to intercept it. Captain Griffin, in charge of a band of men in a Durham boat, along with Adjutant D.W. Church, who was in charge of a gunboat with 18 men and armed with a 6-pounder moved out on September 15 to intercept the enemy bateaux.

The two vessels left Ogdensburg in the evening and by late night had landed on Toussaint Island, located a few miles above Iroquois Point. The Americans quickly captured the only family that lived on the island. However, one family member, a man, managed to slip away and getting in a canoe paddled for the Canadian shore. Captain Griffin, meanwhile took up position with his men at the head of the island, while Church positioned his gunboat at the foot of the island.

The brigade of bateaux, were under the command of Lieutenant and Adjutant of the 49th Regiment of Foot, James FitzGibbon.[73] His force consisted of detachments from the Newfoundland Regiment, the 10th Royal Veterans and the flank company of the 1st Regiment of Dundas Militia under Captain Michael Ault. As the boats neared Toussaint Island on September 16, an officer in the lead bateau thought he spotted a Durham boat. He ordered the men to cease rowing so he could get a better view with his spy glass.

A canoe was soon spotted paddling toward them. The man in the canoe was shouting that there were Americans on the island.

There was no doubt now who the Durham boat belonged to. The bateaux were ordered to head for the north bank. The Americans fired at them as the rowed for shore.

With musket balls whipping by, the bateaux grounded about 20 yards from shore. Soldiers and their wives and children had no choice but to climb over the gunwale of the bateaux and wade to shore. With women screaming and children crying, musket balls continued to splash up water and slam in the boats as the passengers moved as quickly as they could. A sickly wife of an officer stationed at Kingston of considerable girth was hesitant about getting in the water. A portly officer quickly came to her aid, offering to carry her to shore. She accepted and climbed onto his back and they attempted to wade to shore. They didn't make it. The officer began to sink into the mud until he got stuck. He now had no choice to put the lady into the water. Taking her by the hand they manage to get to dry land.[74]

With the passengers safely on shore, the British and Canadians went on the offensive. Part of Captain Ault's company was ferried out to Presqu'isle, where they took up position on the south side of the island. They let loose a deadly volley into the two American vessels that were attempting to land troops on the small island. The Americans pulled back to Toussaint Island, where in the confusion the Durham boat was abandoned and drifted a short piece downstream. It was quickly picked by the Canadian militia. The American gunboat took two volleys from the bateaux headed toward it wounding five of its occupants. The gunboat then brought it's 6-pounder into action, which forced the bateaux to pull back.

Word spread up the north bank of the St. Lawrence like wildfire bringing the militia out. Many began to gather on Presqu'isle. Captains Munroe and Dulmage brought two companies from Grenville along with an old 9-pounder under the command of Lieutenant Richard Duncan Fraser that had been captured from the French back in 1760 on Chimney Island. The old cannon was brought into action firing on the Americans at Toussaint Island. The Americans retreated to their side of the river, while the gunboat proceeded onto Hamilton (modern Waddington, N.Y.). In the little skirmish the Americans suffered 1 killed and 6 wounded, while the British and Canadians had 1 killed and several wounded. The militia did manage to capture seven muskets, two swords and some provisions when they took the Durham boat.[75]

Two days later, Captain Benjamin Forsyth with 90 men from his rifle unit along with 20 New York militiamen under Captain Samuel McNitt headed out of Sackets Harbor for Cape Vincent.[76] Forsyth, a big tough North Carolinian who would not shy away from a fight, did not linger long at Cape Vincent. By nightfall on September 20, he and his men set out in boats bound for Gananoque, located about 17 miles down river from Kingston. This little settlement acted as the last staging point for the bateaux and had a small store of provisions and supplies. Forsyth intended to capture the ammunition stored there and cause alarm on the Canadian side of the river.

Rowing through the Thousand Islands region, the Americans landed their boats a short piece west of Gananoque. Meeting no opposition, Forsyth led his men east toward the small settlement and managed to get within less than a mile when they were discovered. Two horsemen spotted them and one galloped into Gananoque giving the warning of the American presence.

About 110 men of the 2nd Leeds Regiment of Militia, some of them clad in redcoats, formed up to meet Forsyth's raiders.[77] The Upper Canadian militia fired a volley at the Americans. Ignoring the gunfire, Forsyth led his men forward toward the militia line not firing till they were within 100 yards of the enemy. The Leeds militia gave way and ran back to Gananoque where they rallied. Forsyth continued to pursue them and after another brief firefight, forced the Canadians to retreat.

Forsyth's raiders had suffered 1 man killed and 1 wounded. The 2nd Leeds Militia fared worse with 4 wounded and 8 captured. The Americans surrounded the home of the 2nd Leeds commander, Colonel Joel Stone also the founder of Gananoque. Hearing movement upstairs one of the soldiers fired and wounded Mrs. Stone in the hip. They then ransacked the house and attempted to carry of some of the Stone's personnel belongings but were prevented by their officers. Thinking they had killed the Colonel, who was apparently not a home at the time, the soldiers left. Forsyth captured a number of arms, two barrels containing 3,000 ball cartridges, a barrel of flints and another barrel of gunpowder. After torching a storehouse containing some barrels of provisions, Forsyth took his prisoners and returned to his boats. The raid had been very successful.[78]

On October 1, the schooner *Niagara* and some smaller vessels carrying Brigadier General Brown with 320 troops arrived at Ogdensburg. With Brown was Forsyth and his green coated riflemen. General Richard Dodge, commander of the 4th Brigade of New York militia, arrived at Sackets Harbor on September 22 where he outranked Brown. Dodge ordered Brown to Ogdensburg to end the unofficial truce between Ogdensburg and Prescott where a very lucrative trade was occurring. They were not long in town before they began harassing the enemy bateaux. The British and Canadian would soon make an attempt to end this irritant.

The battery at Prescott opened on Ogdensburg on October 2 to cover the approach of 40 bateaux and two gunboats acting as escorts. The bateaux safely rowed into Prescott. Meanwhile the Americans at Ogdensburg began to fire back but to little effect. The following day, the batteries at Prescott continued their bombardment. The Americans did not respond. Not wanting to waste his low supply of gunpowder, Brown instead had his men gather up the spent cannon balls.

Colonel Lethbridge, who had been replaced by Colonel John Vincent at Kingston in mid-August, was now posted at Prescott to take charge of the militia flank companies and oversee the protection of supply convoys moving up river in that area. On October 4, Lethbridge ordered his militia, drawn from Leeds, Grenville and Glengarry counties, into 25 boats for an attempt against Ogdensburg. Two gunboats would support the boats. The guns at Prescott opened up on Ogdensburg, to support the amphibious assault.

Watching the whole process was Brown with a borrowed eyeglass from David Parish. When the Canadian flotilla reached half way across the river, the American guns under D.W. Church and Joseph York opened up. Forsyth's riflemen and the militia under Brown fired on the Canadians with their muskets and rifles.

The hail of lead eventually forced back Lethbridge's force with 3 killed and 4 wounded. The Americans had received no casualties. Lethbridge, who had made the attack without receiving the proper authorization, was relieved of his command.[79] Taking his place was Lieutenant Colonel Thomas Pearson who was also the Inspector of Militia. Irritable and surly, Pearson was a veteran of fighting in Holland, Spain, Egypt, Martinique and Portugal. He was generally disliked by the local militia. At Kingston for example,

Pearson had ripped into Colonel Cartwright for not having his command, the 1st Frontenac Regiment of Militia, perform a movement which a young British officer observing stated that a militia officer "could not be expected to know." Cartwright later commented that Pearson insulted the 1st Frontenac militia more than he did him.[80]

While later stationed at Cornwall, 'Tiger' Dunlop, recounted how a local woman, Peggy Bruce had a run in with Pearson. When Peggy, who was never shy to speak her mind, heard that Pearson was leaving Cornwall she said to him "Och! Colonel dear, and are you going to lave us - sure there will be many a dry eye in the town the day you quit it."[81]

About the same time Pearson arrived, it was determined that a representative of the commissary should be posted at Prescott. Until the representative arrived in the new year, Gilkison, now a captain in the militia, was appointed a clerk in the Commissariat Office. As a merchant he already had been supplying the militia at Prescott.

Further east at St. Regis, Captain McDonnell with a party of Canadian Voyageurs was ordered there by Baynes in mid-October to secure that post and "guard against any predatory incursion on the part of the enemy, to inspire confidence in the Indians of that place and to ensure their good conduct and fidelity." He was to support the Indian Department officer there, Louvigny De Montigny "to insure the respect and prompt obedience of the Indians under his superintendence." Finally if McDonnell could "by stratagem, within the Province line," arrest any American agents "or others endeavoring to mislead the Indians" he was to send them under escort to Montreal. The British were attempting to bring the St. Regis Indians over to their side.[82]

On learning of the Canadian presence at St. Regis, the Americans began to rally to attack them. Major Guilford Dudley Young with a detachment of militia, mostly haling from Troy, New York, marched from French Mills (modern Fort Covington), guided by an Indian interpreter named William Gray. Young's force was unable to attack St. Regis when after reaching the St. Regis River opposite the Indian town, they were unable to find a way to cross the river. They retreated back to French Mills, but not for long.

Late in the evening on October 22, Young led his force again toward St. Regis. At Gray's Mills (modern Hogansburg, New York), Young with 200 men crossed over the river in a boat, canoe and log raft. By 5 A.M. the Americans were at the edge of St. Regis. Young ordered his men to rest behind a small rise west of town while he planned his attack. The Canadians were quartered in two houses in town, one belonging to Montigny and the other McDonnell. The American plan called for three columns to attack the British part of town. Captain Lyon was to take his company and follow a road along the St. Regis River and get in the rear of Montigny's house and a small blockhouse. Captain Tilden with his company was to cut to the west and get behind McDonnell's house and prevent the voyageurs from reaching their boats along the St. Lawrence River. Finally Young would lead the last two companies through the village completing the encirclement of the enemy.

    Young's detachment were within 150 yards of Montigny's house when shooting erupted from the enemy's rear indicating Lyon's company was in position. Lyons's men had been spotted by one of McDonnell's sentinels. A Canadian ensign attempting to escape was ordered to stop by men in Young's detachment. He ignored the command and was shot dead. The fighting soon ended as McDonnell and his voyageurs surrendered. In the little skirmish Young's force suffered no losses, while the Canadians had 7 casualties.

    The Americans took 40 prisoners with their arms, along with a couple of bateaux, stores and a flag. They also found 800 blankets the British had sent to the Indians. Packing up their prisoners and spoils, Young's force headed back to French Mills. The prisoners were sent onto Plattsburg.[83]

    A month later, a Canadian and British force began to gather to retaliate for the American attack on St. Regis. Captain Andrew Gray commanded the force of 250 men made up of a company of Glengarry Light Infantry, a detachment of the Royal Artillery, a handful of soldiers from the 49th Regiment of Foot, as well as the 1st Regiment of the Stormont Militia and the 1st Regiment of Glengarry Militia under Lieutenant Colonel Alexander McMillan. Lieutenant Colonel Neil McLean, commander of the 1st Stormont, superintended the embarkation of the troops.

    There was some debate among the officers of the best route to attack French Mills, the target of the raid. Major 'Red George'

Macdonell and "half the Glengary People" wanted to move up the Salmon River to attack French Mills. They were adamant about this route until Gray finally told them directly that he was in charge of the expedition and they would take the route he had planned. This was the smarter route as they would later discover the Americans had expected an attack up the Salmon River and had posted pickets to ambush any enemy boats moving up river.[84]

Late in the evening on October 21, McLean helped embark the raiders off from Glengarry House. Two hours later the raiders were across the St. Lawrence River and at St. Regis. A detachment from the Glengarry militia were left in the town to prevent any Indians friendly to the Americans from warning them. About 30 pro-British Indians were recruited and the raiders pushed on.

Gray's force wounded the American sentries as they arrived at French Mills and drove the rest of their troops to seek protection in a blockhouse. Gray later reported that the militia "did their Duty with greatest cheerfulness." However he did say: "One of our greatest difficulties was to make them cease firing, and keep their Ranks and be Silent." The company of Glengarry Light Infantry Gray said "conducted themselves remarkably well." Gray however was not overly happy with the Indians as they had drank all the rum before joining the raiders.[85]

A local citizen, who Gray had used as a guide, was sent to the blockhouse to tell the defenders that he was not here "to injure the Persons or properties of individuals" but to retaliate for the raid on the Voyageurs posted at St. Regis. The defenders of the blockhouse surrendered.

While Gray was negotiating the surrender and despite his promise that no private property would be plundered, the Indians ransacked the house of the American aiding Gray's raiders. Gray informed the man he would be compensated for any of his losses. A few other homes nearby were plundered as well as five Americans later applied to the British for compensation, which Prevost recommended they receive.

Gray's raider had bagged 44 prisoners, who as it turned out had not taken part in the St. Regis raid. The raiders had also captured 57 muskets, four bateaux and some military stores. Gray was anxious to be leaving as it was rumored that enemy troops were headed their way. As the captured goods would just slow down Gray's retreat, he ordered the captured muskets and ammunition destroyed and the bateaux sunk in the river. With this done, Gray's raiders with their prisoners retreated. The Americans had suffered possibly as many 7 casualties, while Gray's force did not suffer any. The American prisoners were sent onto Coteau du Lac.[86]

By early November, the American fleet on Lake Ontario had grown to seven vessels and was strong enough that its new commander, Commodore Isaac Chauncey decided to take on the four Provincial Marine vessels. The *Royal George* was spotted on November 9 and the chase began. By the 10th, the pursuit led through the North Channel between Amherst Island and the Bay of Quinte. Chauncey ordered one of his schooners to sail into toward Amherstview to capture a schooner anchored there. The vessel was plundered of its rigging and burned.

As Chauncey's fleet pursued the *Royal George* into Kingston harbor, the militia and regulars at the town quickly mobilized to receive the attackers. Over 1,000 men formed up to await the attack or man the batteries. By mid-afternoon both sides were blazing away at each other with little damage. The fight ended when the American drew off for the night. As they were leaving the Americans managed to capture a Canadian vessel heading into Kingston unaware of the situation there. The Americans had suffered 10 casualties while the British and Canadians had 1 killed.

With the weather turning bad, Chauncey decided not to press another attack against Kingston. As they were heading out for the lake, the Americans spotted a Canadian schooner, the *Governor Simcoe*. Shots were fired her way, but the captain of the schooner knew the waters well and managed to get her into Kingston harbor. Another vessel, the *Elizabeth*, was not so fortunate as it fell into American hands a couple of days later. The year ended well on Lake Ontario for the Americans as they now controlled the lake. Their strength was increased on November 26 when a corvette, the U.S.S. *Madison*, was launched at Sackets Harbor. She was armed with 24 32-pounder carronades.[87]

The war further west in Upper Canada had gone well for the British and Canadians. Fort Michilimackinac, the important post located on Mackinac Island roughly between Lake Huron and Lake

Michigan fell to a combined force of British soldiers, Canadian fur traders, voyageurs and Indians in mid-July. Brock captured Detroit in August 1812. In this bold operation he captured 582 U.S. regulars who were sent east to Quebec City as prisoners, while 1,600 volunteers were paroled. Of great importance to the defenders of Upper Canada was the capture of 33 guns and 2,500 arms. An American invasion was thrown back in mid-October at Queenston Heights. Unfortunately for the British and Canadians, Brock was killed early in the battle. His role was replaced by the Boston born Major General Roger Hale Sheaffe.

CHAPTER 4
BROCKVILLE AND OGDENSBURG
1813

On January 19, 1813, Lieutenant Colonel Ralph Henry Bruyeres of the Royal Engineers reported to Prevost of his inspection of the posts in the upper province. At Prescott, acting on Prevost's orders to have a blockhouse built there, Bruyeres instructed Lieutenant Frederick de Gaugreben, an engineer in the King's German Legion[88], to continue to survey the post there and built a blockhouse "on a small commanding spot" to the rear of the shore battery, earlier constructed by the militia. Work on the new structure would not begin to spring. Across the river at Ogdensburg, Bruyeres five days earlier wrote to the governor on information he had received from American deserters that the troops were disaffected there and were ready to desert because of Forsyth's tyrannical behaviour. He believed the regulars and militia from Prescott could easily take the town, but advised any attack should wait till later in the season when the ice would break up to prevent an American retaliatory action.[89]

Brockville was described by Bruyeres as "the most improved Village on the communication." Brockville he described "has some very handsome Houses with a Church, and Court House, and is situated on an elevated & commanding spot of ground." He went onto say, "there is a small Troop of Cavalry, with a Volunteer Rifle Company and some Militia stationed here; they are however very inefficient, a large proportion of them being absent, and returned to their own homes."

At Gananoque, Bruyeres reported there was a good post there, "with a Company of Militia stationed under the command of Col: Stone." The militia were building a blockhouse "on a strong point of ground near the River." They had the bottom half of the blockhouse up and figured to have the rest completed in about six weeks.

At Kingston, Bruyeres described the state of the Provincial Marine and the new ship to be constructed there. He directed that a blockhouse be "raised and improved" on Point Henry and another constructed on Point Frederick that would protect the dockyard. As soon as the frost came out of the ground he ordered that current batteries be repaired and enclosed. It was of the upmost important that a new powder magazine be built. Currently an old wind mill had been converted into a powder magazine, but Bruyeres thought it to be very dangerous as the mill was surrounded by wooden buildings in the barrack yard. Once the powder was removed to the new magazine, Bruyeres thought a gun could be mounted on the top of the mill.[90]

There were musings of a raid to be launched across the ice against Sackets Harbor, where the Americans were constructing new vessels. Prevost was against the idea and no raid materialized. It would be Forsyth who would attack first, although it would not be Kingston, but further down river at Brockville.

Word from informants had reached the newly promoted Major Forsyth in Ogdensburg that the British had crossed into New York and had captured some deserters as well as American soldiers and civilians. They were being held in the courthouse/jail, described as an elegant brick building, in Brockville. The deserters were said to be sentenced to be executed. Not wasting anytime, Forsyth decided to liberate them.

On February 6, he began to assemble a small force of 200 men. It consisted of his greencoated rifleman, Captain Lydle's company of volunteers and some civilians. At 9 P.M., Forsyth's little force climbed into their sleighs and headed out towards Morrisville (modern Morristown, N.Y.). When they reached this little town, located across the river from Brockville, they got out of their sleighs and prepared to cross the frozen St. Lawrence. Arnold Smith, a local tavern keeper, was recruited to lead them across the river, which was over 2 miles wide here.

Crossing the ice was dangerous as it was not very hard yet. Before crossing, Forsyth divided his force, along with flanking parties. Forsyth took command of one division, while Colonel Benedict of the New York militia took the other division. The flanking parties were commanded by Lieutenants Wells and Johnson.

By 3 A.M. the Americans were ready to move out. Spreading out in open order, so as to reduce their weight on the ice, they crossed over to Brockville unobserved.

Upon reaching the northern bank, the flanking parties took up position at either side of Brockville to cut off any retreat or to check any reinforcements from reaching the town. Forsyth now led the main force through the village toward the courthouse/jail. Adjutant Church was ordered to dispatch small parties to secure various street corners to be in position to prevent any resistance. Forsyth then entered the jail and demanded that the prisoners be released. Sixteen were freed, while one prisoner was left, despite the man's pleas. This man was Sergeant McSween who had been charged with murder. McSween had trouble earlier with Andrew Fuller of the local militia, who had asked the Sergeant permission to go home. McSween denied him, but Fuller said he was going anyway. McSween ordered him to stop, which Fuller just laughed at and kept going. McSween grabbed a musket and shot him, killing Fuller almost instantly. McSween was later tried and sentenced to hang, but was eventually released.[91]

One of the flank companies of the Leeds Regiment of Militia which was posted at the town were captured. Among them was Major Carley, plus three captains and two lieutenants. Prominent citizens of Brockville were also taken prisoner as well. In all about 52 men were taken by Forsyth. The only resistance was one shot fired from a window which slightly wounded one of Forsyth's men. Besides the prisoners, the Americans also captured 120 muskets, 20 rifles, and couple of casks of fixed ammunition and some public stores.

Once across the river, back in Morrisville, Forsyth released one of his prisoners who was a doctor. The rest of the prisoners were taken back to Ogdensburg of which most would be shortly paroled. Forsyth would be promoted to Lieutenant Colonel for his actions.

Sometime later Carley would later be exchanged due to the daring exploits of Captain Reuben Sherwood. A Loyalist, Sherwood in his early teens had served in the Queen's Loyal Rangers late in the Revolutionary War. After taking up his land grant, Sherwood eventually became a surveyor and when war broke out, commanded the 1st Leeds Rifle Company. Knowing the Upper St. Lawrence and northern New York well, Sherwood excelled at gathering intelligence on the enemy. With another officer, Lieutenant Grant, Sherwood and nine men set out to investigate reports that the Americans were building a blockhouse on Gravelly Point, located opposite Wolfe Island at the head of the river.

Sherwood and Grant dropped their men off on an island, while they proceeded on in a small boat. They landed just below the point and headed into the woods. They suddenly came upon American militiamen preparing timbers for a blockhouse. Their muskets lay on the ground. Sherwood demanded to know what they were doing there and to be shown their headquarters. He then added to his bluff by telling Grant to "consider these men prisoners" and gave the ominous warning that if anyone of them attempted to pickup a musket he was to give the Indians the signal. He added only to do so if "absolutely necessary."[92]

Sherwood then went onto the headquarters where he found a major who he demanded his sword and immediate surrender. The American officer believing Sherwood's bluff about the nearby Indians surrendered. Sherwood then paroled the men and sent them home. The major soon learned of the bluff when he was taken to the small boat and eventually onto Prescott. He was exchanged for Carley. More adventures lay ahead for Sherwood.

The same day that Brockville was raided, February 7, Colonel Neil McLean of the 1st Stormont received information of a large American force consisting of 400 regulars, 2000 militia and large numbers of artillery pieces, gathering at Salmon River. He quickly sent the intelligence onto Major General Baron Francis de Rottenberg, who was in command of the Montreal District. De Rottenberg ordered a convoy of 40 sleighs carrying supplies and five 12 pounders guns to stay at Coteau du Lac. McMillian's 1st Glengarry was called out and ordered out to Riviere au Raisin, while McLean was to rally his men at Cornwall in preparation for an American attack.

Pearson upon hearing of Forsyth's raid seemed unconcerned at first as he believed Brockville had no military significance. He did report that with more troops he could take Ogdensburg where the raid originated. No attack was ordered, but tension was mounting between Prescott and Ogdensburg. Some of Forsyth's men raided across the river capturing three Upper Canadian farmers and a team of horses. 'Red George' Macdonell, now at Prescott attempted to negotiate the return of the farmers and their horses but was flatly denied with the Americans adding the threat they would be glad to meet the Canadians on the frozen river to settle the matter. Sergeant James Comins, of the 8th Regiment of Foot, was part of the party sent across the river under a flag of truce. Despite being under the guard of two American soldiers while in Ogdensburg, Comins took stock of the American defences.

On February 21, Prevost arrived at Prescott on an inspection tour of Upper Canada. Pearson quickly advanced the idea of attacking Ogdensburg. Prevost was against the idea preferring things just be left alone. He did agree only to allow Macdonell to make a demonstration on the ice, while he and Pearson, who was to temporarily replace Vincent at Kingston, and the rest of his small group headed onto Brockville.

Two soldiers from the Glengarry Light Infantry had deserted the night before Prevost's arrival and it was feared they had informed the Americans of the Governor's purpose in Upper Canada and his travel rout. Macdonell, now in charge of Prescott, warned Prevost that the Americans might try to intercept him on his journey west. The Governor was having second thoughts of being attacked and send word back to Macdonell that he was not to "undertake any offensive operations against Ogdensburg without previous communications with Major-General de Rottenberg". However, if the Americans did offer an opportunity "for his destruction and that of the shipping, batteries and public stores . . .", Macdonell could attack.[93] The fiery Scot set out to make his own opportunity.

Macdonell's attacking force consisted of about 480 men divided into two columns. The main or east column, which Macdonell would command himself, consisted of about 30 soldiers from the Royal Newfoundland Regiment, 120 men from the 8th Foot, 230 local militia and three guns pulled on sleighs.

The smaller west column was commanded by Captain John Jenkins of the Glengarry Light Infantry. His force consisted of a company of Glengarry Light Infantry, a gun under the command of Lieutenant De Gaugreben and about 70 militia. This column's objective was to cut off the retreat of the Americans. The militia in both columns were drawn from the ranks of the Leeds, Grenville, Dundas, Stormont and Glengarry regiments, bolstered the night before by an inspiration talk from Reverend Macdonell.

At 7 A.M., 'Red George' Macdonell's troops moved onto the ice. A cannon fired to signal the commencement of the assault. Across the river at Ogdensburg, the American sentries watching the British and Canadians troops were not overly alarmed as the soldiers often drilled on the ice. It was only when they were halfway across the ice did the Americans know this was no drill.

From information provided by their spies, the Americans were expecting an attack sometime. Forsyth had written to Dearborn at Plattsburg explaining the impending British attack and requested help. Dearborn could offer no aid but the advice that Forsyth should do what he was able and if he could not hold Ogdensburg, he had permission to abandon it. Dearborn went on to say that if Ogdensburg was lost that it might impassion the American spirit. When Forsyth received Dearborn's response, he called a council of his officers to determine their opinion of the situation. It was decided Ogdensburg would be defended and only abandoned if forced too.

With the decision to hold the town the American set up their defenses. An iron 12-pounder gun under the command of Captain Kellog was positioned close to the intersection of Ford and Euphamia Streets.[94] A brass 6-pounder manned by volunteers and civilians under Joseph York was positioned in front of the arsenal located on the west side of Ford Street. Not far from David Parish's store were the Oswegatchie River emptied into the St. Lawrence, was a wooden breastwork sporting an iron 12-pounder along the river bank, which like the other 12-pounder was captured from the British during the Revolutionary War's Saratoga campaign in1777. It was commanded by Captain Joshua Conkey. A brass 9-pounder mounted on a sled under the command of a sergeant from Kellog's company of the Albany Volunteers was sited across the Oswegatchie River on a point of land jutting out into the St. Lawrence River.

At the back of the old fort leftover from the French regime, or the "stone garrison" as it was known, was two 6-pounders mounted on sleds commanded by Adjutant Church and Lieutenant Baird, one of Forsyth's rifle officers. Placed in front of the gateway, which was between the two buildings that made up the remains of the garrison, was a brass 6-pounder on a sled. An iron 6-pounder was located about 20 feet to the left of the brass one.

Back on the east side of Oswegatchie River, on far side of town was an unfinished redoubt named Fort Oswegatchie. The fort had been laid out by a French engineer who reportedly had seen service under Napoleon. The bulk of the troops defending Ogdensburg were Forsyth's riflemen. There were also a handful of volunteers, but the bulk of the militia had earlier been released to go home.[95]

The American guns opened up on the advancing British and Canadian soldiers. The deep snow slowed down Macdonell's troops exposing them longer to artillery fire, but fortunately for them the firing was mostly high. As Jenkins's column closed in on the "stone garrison" they ran into trouble.

Forsyth paced along his line of his men drawn up at the rear of the old fort facing Jenkins. The first volley of artillery fire was ineffective. When Jenkins's men reached the bank, they came under heavy fire from Forsyth's men. Jenkins urged his men on, but was hit in the left arm by grapeshot from the American's guns. Ignoring the wound he pushed on with his men, when a case shot hit him in the right arm. He continued on a short piece, but quickly went down due to loss of blood and pain. De Gaugreben's gun was disabled, and he headed back to get the militia reserve. Another Glengarry Light Infantry officer, Lieutenant James MacAulay took over, but the column was unable to make any headway against Forsyth and had to give way.

Meanwhile, Macdonell's column, with a company from the Royal Newfoundland Regiment and the volunteer light company of the militia acting as his advance guard under the command of Staff Adjutant Ridge of the 8th Foot were having much more success. Following behind the advance guard were a detachment of the 8th under Captain Eustace and the militia under Colonel Fraser. The American advanced battery hurled grape and cannister at Macdonell's column trudging through the snow. Small arms fire soon joined the cannon fire. Macdonell ordered his advance guard to charge the enemy with their bayonets. Ridge's advance guard took the battery, while the 8th rushed up a parallel street driving off the American infantry posted there and capturing their guns. They then swung one of the guns around and put it to use. A detachment of the militia took over the guns, as the column continued their pursuit of the Americans through the main street to the bridge over the Oswegatchie River. From house windows the British and Canadians were taking "a galling fire". The guns from the old French fort also added to their misery when they reached the high Oswegatchie River bank. It was about this time that Jenkins's attack was driven back.

Here Macdonell halted his men, who by now were out of breath. He lined up the 8th along the bank, "keeping a reserve of Militia in Column". He dispatched small parties on his left flank to dislodge the Americans firing from the houses and woods. With his guns now brought up and under the command of Ensign John McKay of the Glengarry Light Infantry and Ensign John Kerr of the Grenville militia, they were soon firing grape and round shot into the houses to silence the firing coming from them. With that nagging fire silenced, Macdonell ordered his advance guard and a militia company to capture the 12-pounder in the battery near Parish's store.

Before attacking Forsyth, Macdonell sent two men, Lieutenants Richard Duncan Fraser and Jonas Jones to take a message to the American commander at the "stone garrison" offering him the chance to surrender or face the bayonet. Forsyth responded: "Tell Colonel McDonnel there must be more fighting done first." When the messengers had returned back to their own troops, Forsyth had two cannons fire case shot hitting some of the Canadian and British troops.

Macdonell would later report: "I immediately ordered a charge & Captain Eustace with Ensigns Powell & Lowrie (the latter of whom had left a sick bed to join his Company) & his men gallantly rushed on to the charge covered by a three pounder under Ensign Kerr." The yelling of the men prevented them from hearing Macdonell's order to stay on the road that led "to the proper declivity to descend to the River." Macdonell was forced to form the troops into "a better manner with the Company of the Newfoundland & Glengarry Militia, under cover of a large building, & again they pushed on & entered the fort, just as the Enemy had evacuated it on the opposite side & was retiring to the woods." It was then that Macdonell lamented the lack of Indians, which earlier had been sent on escort duty with Prevost, as he could have employed them "in intercepting the Enemy on his retreat & would have captured the whole Garrison." Some Indians did in fact return upon hearing the cannon fire and Macdonell dispatched them in pursuit of the Americans who were driven from the houses and woods, but to little effect.[96]

Forsyth quickly ordered a retreat to Thurber's tavern, where his men rendezvoused and continued onto De Peyster Corners. In the battle Forsyth suffered over 20 casualties. Macdonell would report that he took 70 prisoners, many of which would be paroled. Not having enough men to make an attempt to recapture Ogdensburg, Forsyth wrote to the secretary of war reporting the loss of the town and adding: "If you can send me three hundred men, all shall be retaken, and Prescott too, or I will lose my life in the attempt." There would be no attempt by Forsyth. Brown, leading a relief force, met up with Forsyth at Black River and ordered him to retreat to Sackets Harbor. Brown headed onto Ogdensburg.[97]

Macdonell's force suffered 7 killed and 63 wounded, including the Lieutenant-Colonel himself. Jenkins was severely wounded and would end up losing an arm. He would spend the rest of the war as town major of Fredericton, New Brunswick.[98] After securing his position in Ogdensburg, Macdonell ordered his troops to carry "off all the Ordnance, Commissariat & the Marine stores, and a quantity of camp equipage & clothing." The ordnance they captured was considerable - 11 canons. They also took 672 stand of arms, 12 barrels of powder, 14 kegs of cartridges. Two gunboats were torched as were two schooners. The old and new barracks were also burned.[99] Government stores were not the only thing taken.

"I did not leave the house until the British were close to it, and not till they had shot a great number of balls into it. I took nothing with me but some money, and my table spoons, and ran as fast as possible, with a number of other woman," wrote Mrs. York, a resident of Ogdensburg. She was like many other residents who fled as the battle raged into their town. They were to find a rude shock when they finally returned to their homes. "The next day I returned; our house was plundered of almost of everything, and my husband a prisoner on the other side. They did not leave any article of clothing, not even a handkerchief - they took all my bedding but left the beds; they broke my looking glasses and even my knives." She managed to procure the release of her husband who was paroled, but had little success in getting back their stolen property. Her husband was a well-known partizan and this may have made their house a specific target, but Mrs. York did comment that "most of the houses in the village were plundered." She leveled the blame not only at the Indians and soldiers who plundered during the battle, but the "women on the other side" who came across when the fighting was over "and took what was left."[100]

David Parish's store was also looted. Joseph Rosseel commented on the looting: "At one time they were carrying off some of my property and hurrying my person off to Canada when a British officer who knew me, happening to pass my house, perceiving my embarrassment, rushed in, bid the ruffians desist and dispersed them."[101] It was not only Upper Canadians doing the plundering, some Americans also joined in. Parish a few months later was smoothing things over with the British at Prescott making sure his business would continue. Besides helping the American government to float a war loan of $16,000,000, Parish and another Ogdensburg merchant would by the end of the year help supply the British and Canadians at Prescott for the rest of the war.

After the battle, prisoners were released from jail claiming they were being held for political reasons. After it was discovered their true reasons for being in jail, some of them were recaptured and turned over to the sheriff.

Brown with his relief force arrived in Ogdensburg a few days later. He ordered any provisions not taken by Macdonell to be loaded on a sleigh and taken to Sackets Harbor. Brown later recommended troops be posted at the river town. Nothing would come of it. The citizens of Ogdensburg requested their government not to post troops in their town. Macdonell thought that Parish helped in this, as his property was at 'Red George's' mercy. American troops, however, would be at Ogdensburg during the Wilkinson campaign in the fall of 1813.

Prevost who was at Kingston when he heard of Macdonell's attack on Ogdensburg wrote to him stating: "Although you have rather exceeded my orders, I am well pleased with what you have done . . .."[102] Dearborn besides sending out Brown, ordered 800 regular troops to travel from Plattsburg to Sackets Harbor fearing it would be attacked next. Chauncey who originally believed the attack on Ogdensburg was designed to strength the British hold on Prescott, began to fear by March an attack was imminent on Sackets Harbor as well. Eventually the fear would subside with the breaking of the ice and reinforcements strengthening the American naval base.

Some of this alarm was caused by a number of regular troops being sent upriver into Upper Canada. Although the Americans were getting reports of exaggerated numbers, it was true Prevost was sending more troops into Upper Canada.

Besides troops being sent into the province, attempts were made to raise three regiments for the new "Volunteer Battalion of Incorporated Militia" which was to replace the flank companies. The men recruited for the unit would serve for the duration of the war. Recruiting in the Eastern District was under Colonel Neil McLean. In the Johnstown District, Lieutenant Colonel Levius Sherwood was recruiting. In the middle of May, 1813, the companies recruited in the two districts were combined at Prescott, with Levius Sherwood being in command. There were now six companies numbering 329 men. At Kingston, three companies were formed.

Besides infantry, two provincial dragoons unit were raised in the Johnstown and Eastern Districts. One was under command of Captain Andrew Adams. The other one under the command of Richard Duncan Fraser who was promoted to captain in the 1st Dundas Regiment of Militia on February 25, although it would be a year before it was officially issued. Originally, Fraser was a lieutenant in the 2nd Grenville Regiment of Militia where he commanded a gun at Toussaint Island and Ogdensburg. Fraser's father, Thomas Fraser, a former Loyalist captain in Jessup's Loyal Rangers was now a Lieutenant-Colonel in command of the 1st Dundas. Richard Fraser was born in 1784 in Quebec and grew up in Edwardsburg Township where his father settled. In 1802, Fraser when to work as a clerk for the North West Company and was posted at Lake Nipigon. Five years later he was back in Edwardsburg where he claimed his 200 acre land grant for being the son of a Loyalists. He settled in Johnstown not far from Prescott, where he operated as a merchant.

Recruiting for the two dragoons units began in March and went very well. By May, Adams and Fraser's dragoons consisted of the two captains, four subalterns, six sergeants and 100 troopers. The numbers would be cut back eventually amalgamating into one troop under Fraser in early September. The dragoons were poorly equipped for much of 1813 with many of them forced to ride bareback. Uniforms and cavalry equipment were ordered for them, but were slow in coming. The dragoons primary role would be as acting as express riders and patrolling. They would operated out of 18 stations along the Upper St. Lawrence with the headquarters being at Prescott where 12 men would be stationed.[103]

There were other changes made in 1813 on the St. Lawrence River. The Corps of Canadian Voyageurs was replaced in early April with the Corps of Commissariat Voyageurs. This new establishment had 13 officers, 10 sergeants and 400 men who were to serve for 18 months or until the war ended. Pay was to be equal to that of the militia and there was to be additional pay for each voyage from Lachine to Kingston and back. The "Head and Stern Men" were to get 40 shillings, while the "Middle Men", which to there were to be three to a bateau, received 30 shillings. There was to be a bounty of 40 shillings for the men "to furnish themselves with small Necessaries on entering, and be provided with suitable clothing for service." At the end of the transportation season the men were to be allowed to return home and were required to be back on duty by April 20. During their winters off, they would not be paid. The unit was to be commanded by senior officers in the commissariat, Isaac Clarke and John Finlay. Headquarters was to be at Lachine.[104]

Beside more troops coming into or being raised in Upper Canada, Prevost on February 8 had divided Upper Canada into three areas of command. Amherstburg was one area in the western portion of the province, the second area encompassed the territory west of Prescott to Fort George along the Niagara River. Vincent, now a brigadier general, was to command here. The third area was the Upper St. Lawrence from Prescott to Lower Canada where Pearson was in command.[105]

CHAPTER 5
SACKETS HARBOR
1813

One of the most remarkable marches of the war took place in the winter of 1813. The 104th Regiment of Foot (formerly the New Brunswick Fencibles until 1811 when the unit volunteered to become a line regiment) was ordered by Prevost to march from New Brunswick to Lower Canada. Starting out on February 16th the troops moved out from Fredericton in Indian file, broken up into squads with a certain number of toboggans issued to each squad. The last troops left Fredericton on the 21st. Trudging through deep snow on snowshoes and enduring severe cold, the troops reached Quebec City in the middle of March. From there they were ordered onto Montreal and then Kingston where they arrived on April 12. They had marched over 700 miles.[106]

Others units or elements of units were sent upriver as well. The Canadian Voltigeurs, raised in Lower Canada had four companies under Major Frederick Heriot ordered to Kingston on March, 20. A company of the Royal Scots (1st Regiment of Foot) was ordered to Prescott to relieve two companies of the 8th which would then head onto Kingston.[107] More troops were on their way to Upper Canada.

"The 1st Brigade of the Line, and the 1st Demi Brigade of Light Infantry, with a Car Brigade of Light Artillery" were ordered to proceed to Kingston "in light marching Order". Their baggage that was not "indispensably requisite to preserve the comfort and health of the troops" was to be shipped by bateaux under a small guard. The troops were "to carry their great Coats", while their blankets were to be "packed in Bales and sent in Boats." The troops were to move "by Column of Grand Divisions, of two Companies each, to follow in daily succession". From Lachine the soldiers would travel by bateaux to the Cedars, where they would disembark and march "Six Miles above Coteau du Lac, where they will embark in the Second Division of Boats and proceed to Cornwall, untill they arrive where the road becomes good." The troops would continue on by land, while the bateaux would return "to bring on the following divisions of Troops." The Royal Artillery was ordered to take their horses overland from Coteau du Lac to Cornwall, while their guns would be transported by water. Also headed to Kingston was the 98th Foot and the 2nd battalion of the 41st Foot, both fresh from the West Indies.[108]

Captain Jacques Viger of the Voltigeurs, a newspaper editor before the war and author of a book on Louis XVI, left a descriptive account of Kingston in the spring of 1813. "The town stands on the site of old Fort Frontenac," he wrote adding that it was "on a point of land . . . the streets lie mostly at right angles, and are straight and wide." On the eastern edge of town were the barracks and the King's storehouse. "The barracks, built partly of stone and partly of wood, are two storeys high; they face a square." He described the tower still being used as a powder magazine, as well as the artillery barracks and two large buildings in the middle of town that were "used as a military hospital."

He goes on to say that "Kingston is divided into two portions by a central square, which is used as a parade-ground for the troops." Forming part of the square was a wooden market building and an Anglican Church. "To the right of the square" was the court-house and Walker's Hotel which were both stone and two storeys high. A Roman Catholic Church constructed of stone was in Kingston, but its interior was unfinished and was serving as a public hospital. An old wooden house moved from a nearby island served as 'The Commandant's House'."

"To the west is Point Mississauga, and still farther west is Point Murray," wrote Viger describing the naval and military defences of Kingston. "These two important points have been fortified; batteries have been erected there. The first is faced with heavy squared timber. In the rear of the town, and on the right flank, have been erected several redoubts, part of stone and part of wood . . .."

Viger described the bay, which ran for five miles or so to the north and to which the Cataraqui River emptied into, as a fine harbour "where vessels can be secured most comfortably for wintering." The eastern shore was cut into three points. The farthest was Point Hamilton and heavily wooded. Off its shore was Cedar Island recently having its trees cleared. Here sat the telegraph station which had a good view out onto the lake as well as other telegraph stations. These telegraph stations communicated with each other through visual signaling by the use of a mast with an upper and lower yard arms on which were run up flags and balls.

"The middle point is Point Henry," explained Viger, "which has been cleared of wood, with the object of planting there a camp of observation. It is proposed to erect here extensive fortifications." The closest point was Point Frederick. "It is a very level piece of ground, low-lying and well fortified, occupied by the naval buildings, yard and Admiralty buildings. Between Points Frederick and Henry lay Navy Bay. "The security of Kingston on the water side depends on the co-operation of the batteries of Point Frederick and Mississauga Point; and the cross-firing from these two points, if well directed, should make the entrance of the harbour an impossibility."[109]

At the end of April, Viger described the alarm being sounded at midnight, when it was heard that York fell to the Americans. It was feared that the Americans would attempt to cut off Sheaffe's defeated army retreating to Kingston. On May 1st another alarm was given as it was reported that the American fleet was seen sailing toward Kingston. No attack materialized, although the capture of Kingston was a goal of the Americans.[110]

The new secretary of war, John Armstrong, who took up his position in January of 1813 favored the idea that blocking the St. Lawrence River should be the main objective of the American forces for the coming year. In 1812, while a private citizen, Armstrong wrote to the then secretary of war on the importance of the St. Lawrence: "In invading a neighboring and independent territory like Canada, having a frontier of immense extent; destitute of means strictly its own for the purpose of defense; separated from the rest of the empire by an ocean, and having to this but one outlet - this outlet forms your true object or point of attack."[111]

On February 10, Armstrong wrote to Dearborn to mass 4,000 troops at Sackets Harbor, with another 3,000 at Buffalo. The troops at Sackets Harbor were to move by boat, escorted by the navy, to attack Kingston as soon as the navigation season opened. After taking Kingston, the American forces were to take York and capture or destroy the ships reported to being constructed and repaired there. Finally they were to join the troops at Buffalo for invasion of the Niagara region.

Dearborn was not happy with Armstrong's plan and with the help of Chauncey hoped to get it altered. He advised the Secretary of War that York should be captured first, where the capture or destruction of the vessels there would give Chauncey control of Lake Ontario. After York was taken, the troops should then join with the forces at Buffalo and take Forts Erie and George along the Niagara River. Finally the combined force could then move onto Kingston, which they believed was heavily reinforced. Armstrong agreed to the changes and the campaign of 1813 moved away from the St. Lawrence River.[112]

York fell on April 27, with heavy casualties for the Americans. They managed to capture the *Duke of Gloucester* which was being repaired, while the new ship being built, the *Sir Isaac Brock*, was burned by the British. The ship captured by the Americans was later renamed the *York*. Sheaffe retreated back to Kingston, while the Americans moved onto take Fort George a month later.

While this was happening, Samuel Stacy from Ogdensburg who was working for the British, had gone to Sackets Harbor and found out information on the American fleet and the situation there.[113] He quickly headed to Kingston to reveal the information he collected. Prevost, who was at Kingston, received more information on May 26 that Fort George under Major General John Vincent was being bombarded and that a large American force reported to compose of 8,000 regulars, volunteers and militia was preparing to attack it. Prevost ordered the new commodore and commander in chief of the Royal Navy on the inland lakes, Sir James Lucas Yeo, to investigate Sackets Harbor to confirm the information he received on the American naval base.[114] In early 1813, the Royal Navy took over control of the lakes from the Provincial Marine. In late March, 447 Royal Navy officers and seamen arrived at Quebec City to take command and bolster the navy on the lakes.[115]

Yeo on his return to Kingston on May 27, verified that the American fleet was not at Sackets Harbor. Prevost and his senior officers decided to attack. With "the situation of Upper Canada becoming extremely critical, I determined in attempting a diversion in Col. Vincent favor, by embarking the principal part of the small Garrison at this place and proceeding with them to Sacketts Harbour", wrote Prevost to Lord Bathurst, Secretary for War and the Colonies, on June 1 after hearing of the cannonading of Fort George[116]

The troops who were to take part in operation were assembled quickly. The grenadier company of the 100th Foot, a section of the 1st Regiment of Foot, two companies from the 8th Foot and two 6-pounders with gunners were assembled, while the British North American units contributed four companies from the 104th Foot, one company of the Glengarry Light Infantry, two companies of the Canadian Voltigeurs and about 40 Mississauga and Mohawk warriors. A detachment of the Royal Newfoundland Regiment were already aboard the Royal Navy ships serving as marines. In all there were about 900 troops, the majority being British North Americans. Colonel Baynes was given command of the troops.[117]

The troops loaded into 33 bateaux and small crafts and set out from Kingston around sunset to join the ships anchored at the mouth of the harbour. Yeo had about 700 sailors to man his Royal Navy vessels; *Wolfe, Royal George, Earl of Moria, Beresford* and *Sir Sidney Smith* and three gun boats. A merchant vessel, the *Lady Murray* carried the two artillery pieces and some infantry.[118] Those troops not fortune enough to be taken aboard the naval vessels were forced to stay aboard the bateaux due to lack of space on the ships.

A strong cool breeze pushed the ships towing the bateaux toward Sackets Harbor which was about 36 miles away. Around 2 A.M. the breeze slackened somewhat slowing down the armada considerably. A little after dawn, Sackets Harbor was finally spotted. Captain Gray climbed into a canoe and headed in to have a better look at Sackets Harbor. Yeo, in a gig, also reconnoitered the enemy's defences. Guarding Sackets were Fort Volunteer, Fort Tompkins and guns positioned on Navy Point. The lake town also had a basswood cantonment, blockhouse and barracks. The garrison consisted of 947 officers and men from the 1st Light Dragoons, Albany Volunteers, artillerymen as well soldiers from various regiments who were hospitalized at Fort Volunteer. The garrison was under the command of Colonel Electus Backus. By 9 A.M., Gray was back with information that Sackets Harbor looked like it was weakly held.[119]

 Major William Drummond of the 104th, ordered his men into the bateaux "to practice pulling", but in reality he intended to head towards shore. Prevost ordered him back and to re-embark his men back aboard the vessel they were on.[120] The fleet was still about 7 miles from Sackets Harbor slowed by the dying wind.

 Suddenly three American schooners, *Fair American, Pert* and *Lady of the Lake*, were spotted. The last schooner quickly made its way toward the American fleet offshore from Fort George to give warning of the British presence. The other two vessels headed for Sackets Harbor firing their guns to give warning.

 Sackets Harbor now bustled with activity. A messenger was sent to Brown at his home, telling him of the British presence. He quickly headed into town to take charge of the American defences. Messengers were sent out to rally the militia as well as to hurry up a couple hundred soldiers of the 9th U.S. Infantry who were marching toward Sackets Harbor. About 250 more regular troops under the command of Major Thomas Aspinwall were also heading to Sackets, but they were traveling by bateaux from Oswego.[121]

 Prevost meanwhile had decided to call off the attack due to the wind coming from the direction the armada was headed. Shortly afterwards the British spotted Aspinwall's bateaux. Brown and Backus watching from shore figured Aspinwall's bateaux would make Sackets before the British could reach them or at least they would head for shore when they spotted the British fleet. They figured wrong.

 The Indians set out after the American convoy in their fast moving canoes, along with the Glengarry Light Infantry in a gunboat. They opened up on the Americans when they began to close in on their bateaux. Aspinwall's men panicked and began rowing madly for shore where they hoped to take to the woods. The Indians quickly followed them into the forest where fighting ensued. The Americans were getting the worse of it suffering about 35 casualties. A 115 of the U.S. troops made their were back to their bateaux and pushed off heading for the British ships where they surrendered. The remaining American soldiers managed to make their way back to their own lines. The Indians had suffered one killed and one warrior mortally wounded.[122]

 Brown figured the British would attempt a landing on or

near Horse Island. Located west of town, the island was connected to the main land by a narrow partially submerged causeway. He ordered the roughly 600 men of the militia along with a 6-pounder to take up position behind a gravel embankment facing the causeway. On the island itself, Brown ordered the Albany Volunteers under the command of Colonel John Mills to take position there. They also had a 6-pounder with them. If attacked and forced to give away, the militia and volunteers were to harass the British and Canadian's flank.

About 313 dismounted dragoons along with a little over 140 regulars from 9th, 21st and 23rd Infantry Regiments, supported by 6-pounder, were formed up in a ditch in front of Basswood Cantonment west of town. A thick woods separated them from the militia and volunteers. Aspinwall and his men who survived the fight with the Indians reinforced the American lines while mounted dragoons were stationed near the Basswood Cantonment. Should the British push through the American defenders, they were to fall back to Fort Volunteer to make a stand. Meanwhile, the navy stores and the schooners upon such an event, were to be burned by the navy contingent manning the guns at Navy Point.

The 1,450 militia and regular now defending Sackets Harbor would see no British attack on the 28th, but they would the following day. Prevost, after consultation with his senior officers, decided to attack the American naval base, despite his earlier decision to call off the attack. One of Prevost's provincial aides-de-camp wrote that the decision was made due to the capture of the Aspinwall's convoy which "depriving the enemy of part of the intended reinforcements and marking so clearly the description of people we had to contend with . . .." The wind had also become "favourable for reaching the harbour" as well.[123] The attack was scheduled to take place at dawn.

It was around 1 A.M. when the bateaux loaded with British and Canadians troops were formed up in a "compact and regular order". Baynes would report a day later:

"it was intended to remain until the day broke, in the hope of effecting a landing before the Enemy could be prepared to line the Woods with Troops, which surrounded the Coast, but unfortunately a strong current drifted the Boats considerably, while the darkness of the night and ignorance of the Coast prevented them from recovering the proper Station."[124]

By 3:30 A.M. the bateaux began being rowed toward shore, escorted by gunboats and the *Beresford*. First light revealed the boats to the Americans. A militia officer watching the troop laden bateaux commented to his men, "I fear we shall be compelled to retreat." He continued, "I know we shall, and as I am a little lame, I'll start now."[125]

Originally the British and Canadians were to land in the cove formed by Horse Island. Heavy small arms and field artillery fire from the Albany Volunteers began to take its toll on the British and Canadian troops forcing them to head theirs boats for the north side of the island. Some of the gunboats, meanwhile, moved in and began to blast the island. The bateaux still continued to take fire not only from the Americans on the island, but also from the big 32-pounder at Fort Tompkins which added misery to the British and Canadian troops.[126]

The grenadiers of the 100th Foot splashed ashore first onto Horse Island. The Albany Volunteers had by this time retreated back to the mainland and taken up position to the right of the militia. More British and Canadian troops began to land. An unfortunate friendly fire incident occurred when the Voltigeurs, who moved toward the firefight at the causeway, fired into the backs of the 104th hitting eight of their men. Major Drummond quickly ran toward the Lower Canadian unit yelling at them what had happened. Captain Viger made sure there was no second volley.

The 100th rushed across the causeway in a bayonet charge which routed the militia, who managed to fire a few volleys then to Brown's astonishment broke. The American commander desperately tried to rally his men but to no avail. The Albany Volunteers stood their ground and poured three or four volleys into the advancing redcoats. Realizing the militia had fled, the Volunteers retreated as well joining up with the dismounted dragoons and regulars. It was during the retreat that the Volunteers's commander, Colonel Mills, was killed. About 80 or so militiamen were rallied under Captain Samuel McNitt and took cover behind some logs and poured fire into the attackers.[127]

Pushing back the Americans, an unarmed Yeo dressed in round jacket and waving his cap encouraged the troops on.

Drummond sword in hand, was at the forefront as well. An American soldier took aim at Drummond, waiting till he about 20 yards away then fired. Drummond went down. His men quickly bayoneted the American. "Tis not mortal, I can move my legs," said Drummond as his troops lifted him up. "Charge on Men!" Drummond was lucky. Earlier in the day he had been encouraged to remove his epaulettes which he tucked into the front pocket of his overalls. It was hear the ball struck the pad and steel plate of his epaulettes. He was bruised but still alive.[128]

Once across the causeway, Baynes divided his force. Colonel Young of the 8th Foot was ordered to take half the detachment and push on along the road that ran along the lake toward Sackets Harbor. Drummond was to take part of the 104th, Voltigeurs and Indians and follow a path to the right. The British and Canadians had no field artillery support. Although they had captured the American 6-pounder when they drove off the militia, they had no artillerymen to man the gun as they had yet to disembark from the schooner with their own guns.[129]

The terrain the British and Canadian moved into was a mixture of felled trees forming an abatis, underbrush, open fields and woods. Dislodging the Americans proved difficult and had to be done with the bayonet. It was about to get harder as Backus ordered in some of his regulars to check the advance of the British and Canadians.

The fighting intensified as Baynes's troops bumped into the American regulars. Men began to drop as the outnumbered Americans started to withdraw back. The British and Canadian regulars pushed them hard, but the U.S. troops did not break making a stand in the ditch near the Basswood Cantonment. The 32-pounder from Fort Tompkins gave them support as did infantry fire from the palisaded barracks. East of the causeway, McNitt and his men still held out. Brown appeared on the scene, urged them to hang on and rode of to find reinforcements for them, but returned shortly afterwards empty handed. Brown and McNitt's little command now headed toward where the regulars held out. After bumping into the British, some of the McNitt's men managed to move on and join up with Backus. Brown meanwhile rode off to rally more troops.[130]

Although the British and Canadians were getting some support from their gunboats, most of the larger vessels were of little help due to lack of wind. The American's regular stand in front of the Cantonment was stalling Baynes's advance and inflicting casualties. Baynes sought advice from Prevost who was with the troops. It was decided to regroup and make another attempt at the American's positions. Forming up, there was about 300 British and Canadians available to make the assault.

The U.S. regulars and dragoons ranks were thinning too, and Backus decided to pull his men back to Fort Volunteer. Before it was done he was mortally wounded and command of the professional troops fell to Major Jacint Laval. The troops retreated through Sackets heading for Fort Volunteer. A valiant defense continued at the blockhouse supported by Aspinwall's men.[131]

The British and Canadians took the Cantonment and torched the barracks, but could not take the blockhouse. One of the captured guns at the barracks was captured by a major and lieutenant and his servant of the 104th. They attempted to turn the guns on the blockhouse but the major and servant were wounded. Suddenly a bugle could be heard signaling the order to retreat. The troops began to fall back and form up out of range of the blockhouse.[132]

". . . [A]t this point the further energies of the Troops became unavailing - their Block House and Stockaded Battery, could not be carried by assault," later reported Baynes.[133] Prevost sent Drummond toward the Americans holding the blockhouse under a white flag to demand them to surrender. They refused and Prevost decided not to renew the assault. With no field artillery and already suffering heavy casualties, Prevost ordered a retreat to end the bloodshed.

Ironically, the Royal artillery contingent was just unloading their guns when Prevost's decided to retreat. Dust clouds spotted rising from the other end of town may have caused some of the British to believe American reinforcements were arriving.

While most of the American troops retreated from Sackets Harbor, reports reached Lieutenant John Drury of the United States Navy, who was in charge of the batteries on Navy Point, that the battle was lost and Fort Tompkins had fallen. Lieutenant Wolcott Chauncey, brother of the Commodore who was in charge of the naval base, had earlier ordered Drury to torch the naval storehouses and spike the guns to avoid them being captured if things went badly.

Chauncey, who boarded the *Fair American*, would raise and lower a red flag on his vessel to signal Drury to destroy the naval stores. Now as it seemed all was lost in Sackets, a red flag was spotted flying and then lowered on the *Fair American*.[134] The guns were spiked and the naval stores and buildings were set on fire. Sparks and flames soon began to threaten the new vessel being built, *General Pike*, still in her stocks. Drury and his men then headed by boat for Fort Volunteer, when Chauncey hailed in him to explain his actions. Just then the *Beresford* came into view and Chauncey ordered his vessels to fire on her. Back on shore, Major Samuel Brown, Jacob Brown's brother, organized a fire brigade and extinguished the fire that was threatening the *General Pike*.

Many of the British and Canadians retreating were not happy to be leaving. Baynes report that the retreat "was preformed at our leisure and in perfect order" but this was not entirely true.[135] One officer said many of the soldiers "made off as fast as they could".[136] A rumored cavalry pursuit hurried many of the British and Canadian soldiers along. A small American force did follow after the British and Canadians but did not make contact with them.

With the tired and hungry troops back aboard the ships and bateaux, the British fleet headed back to Kingston. Casualties were heavy for the British and Canadians. They suffered 192 wounded, 48 killed and 16 missing - about a quarter of their soldiers. "It was a scandalously managed affair. We gained a surprise and threw it away to allow the enemy to gain time. The murmurs against Sir George were deep, not loud," wrote Lieutenant John Le Couteur of the 104th of the failed attack.[137] The Americans on the other hand lost 21 killed, 85 wounded and 26 missing. They also had 150 men captured the day before the battle with the capture of part Aspinwall's command.[138]

CHAPTER 6
BEGINNING OF WILKINSON'S CAMPAIGN
1813

On the Niagara peninsula, the Americans captured Fort George, but shortly afterwards their invasion stalled with the British night attack at Stoney Creek on June 6. Another American expedition sent out later that month also ended in disaster at Beaver Dams. For the rest of the year the American troops were bottled up at Fort George until December when they retreated back into New York.

Sheaffe was replaced by Major General Baron Francis de Rottenburg in June. The new commander had been born in Danzig, Poland in 1757. In 1782 he joined the army of Louis XVI of France. He left it nine years later to return to Poland and join in their fight for independence from Russia. With the Polish defeat at Warsaw in 1794, De Rottenburg joined the British army the following year. De Rottenburg would see service in Ireland, the West Indies and in 1809 he would take part in the Walcheren Campaign. The author of a manual called *Regulation for the Exercise of Riflemen and Light Infantry and Instructions for their Conduct in the Field,* De Rottenburg came to Lower Canada in 1810 and two years later was in command of the Montreal District.[139]

De Rottenburg, now in Upper Canada, quickly began to reorganize the division of command in the province. The Right Division in western Upper Canada was under the command of Major General Henry Proctor. The Centre Division, under the command of Vincent, now ran from York to the Niagara River, while the Left Division extended from Kingston to the Lower Canada border.

In June a troop of the 19th Light Dragoons were ordered to Kingston. They were followed by the whole regiment the following month. It is interesting to note the trouble the dragoons had in getting their mounts into Upper Canada. It was very much a mud march. A couple of miles above Coteau the regiment's oats and baggage were loaded on a bateau to bypass the road which passed through a swamp that was impossible for wheeled vehicles to move through. It was hard enough for the horses, in fact at one place the swamp was so bad that the troopers had to take their horses out into the river and swim them for a quarter of a mile to avoid sinking in the mud. For six miles they traveled through the water, which in itself was dangerous with roots and half-submerged timbers. Back on land they traveled another eight miles through swampy woods, which at some points the horses were up to their bellies in mud. If this was not bad enough for the troopers and horses, both men and beasts were pelted with rain.[140]

Lieutenant John Lang of the 19th had little love for the inhabitants of the Upper St. Lawrence. When he reached Lancaster, at the mouth of the River Raisin, he referred to it as "the first Yankee town" they had reached. At "Somers" Tavern in Lancaster, Lang found himself and his fellow troopers unwelcome. He claimed that the landlady tried to rob the colonel of $16 from his clothes that were drying by the fire. Lang was not impressed with Upper Canada nor its inhabitants referring to them as "Yankees". On the march to Kingston he stated that the dragoons found themselves "in a hostile country." They slept in their clothes for the people in the area he said where from the United States, "very much disaffected" who had regular communication with the Americans.[141]

When the troopers reached Prescott, they would have found the place bustling with activity. Work on the new fortification well under way. Jessup's orchard was destroyed so as not to give the Americans any cover should they attack. Two of his buildings were tore down as well. The blockhouse being constructed was to be a 100 feet by 100 feet. A 100 cords of stone were needed for the foundation alone. Fortunately for De Gaugreben there was a quarry on Jessup's property. By late June the earthworks were advancing well and two powder magazines were completed. De Gaugreben believed the whole work would be done in three months. Pearson on the other hand was more realistic when he wrote in August that he believed the work would not be finished in 1813. He was right.[142]

The troopers might have also found Prescott alarmed at the American capture of a brigade of bateaux. Privateers began operating out of Sackets Harbor in early July. Two vessels, the *Neptune* carrying a 6 pounder and the *Fox* armed with an 18 pounder, set out from the American naval base for a cruise on the St. Lawrence. The first vessel was under the command of Major Dimock while the later vessel was commanded by Captain Dixon. They stopped at Cape Vincent and then pushed onto French Creek (modern Clayton, N.Y.), finally taking up position among the Thousand Islands, roughly half way between Gananoque and Prescott. From there two smaller boats were rowed out to watch for the enemy.[143]

At 4 A.M., on July 19th, the Americans surprised and captured 15 Canadian bateaux along with their escort gunboat, the *Spitfire,* without casualties. The privateers captured 300 bags of "pilot bread", 270 barrels of Irish pork, military supplies, a 12-pounder carronade and 67 prisoners. The Americans then headed for Goose Creek (also referred to as Cranberry Creek) located across from Wellesley Island, about 40 miles or so upriver from Ogdensburg.

Upon hearing of the capture of the supply convoy at Kingston, three gunboats under the command of Lieutenant John Scott, RN (Royal Navy) were dispatched to pass by the south side of the river in hopes of intercepting the privateers. Meanwhile a detachment of soldiers from the 100th Foot under the command of Captain John Martin would travel by the northern channel. The two parties joined together below Wolfe Island. They soon learned that the Americans were at Goose Creek and quickly headed there. Darkness ended any thoughts of attack, so Scott and Martin took up position for the night at the mouth of the creek. It was here they were joined by Major Richard Frend and a large detachment of redcoats from the 41st Foot from Prescott. Frend took command of the combined force.

At 3 A.M., the following day the British headed up the creek hoping to reach the Americans by dawn. It was soon discovered that the privateers had taken their vessels several miles further up the creek. As the creek narrowed, the gunboats crews were soon unable to use their oars. Progress was also hampered by large trees that the Americans had fallen across the creek. The American also had another surprise for the British. They had built a breastwork out of the barrels of pork and bags of hard bread. As the British attempted to remove the fallen trees, they took fire from a gun in the American "pork-and-bread fort" as one person from Sackets described the breastwork, as well as from the Americans vessels. Muskets flashed and crashed from the thick woods along the left bank of the creek.

British troops had been disembarked on the right side of the creek, but found it impracticable to move on the privateer's position. They returned to the boats in the rear and attempted to cross to the other side of the creek, but due to the swampy terrain could not find a place to land. The lead boat meanwhile was taking heavy fire, dropping many of her crew which checked the fire of her gun, the only one on of all the boats that could be brought to aim on the privateers. Lieutenant Fawcett of the 100th and his men, meanwhile, jumped into the water and holding their muskets and cartridge boxes on their heads, waded to shore and drove the Americans back to their makeshift fort.

A British officer with a flag demanded the surrender of the fort with the bluff of reinforcements being brought up and letting loose the Indians upon them. No quarter would be given if this happened. Dimock replied that there would be no surrender. Frend decided to call of the attack. With the American privateers well positioned in their breastwork and with the gunboats not being able to provide support, Frend broke off the fight not wanting to lose any more men. As it was, he had 4 soldiers killed and 12 wounded. A midshipman and 4 seamen were also wounded in the fray. The Americans had 3 killed and 1 wounded.

With the British gone, the privateers headed their vessels back for the St. Lawrence River. There they found the *Earl of Moria* and her 18 guns waiting for them. The Americans managed to get past the Royal Navy ship, but not before the *Fox* passed within half a musket shot of the *Earl of Moria* and took three hits, one of which passed through her magazine, but did no serious damage. The privateers made it back to Sackets Harbor safely.[144]

It was about this time, July 21, that Yeo was writing to Prevost from the *Wolfe* anchored at Kingston on a scheme for a flotilla of gunboats to operate on the St. Lawrence River to protect the supplies moving upriver. His plan called for nine gunboats, which would be divided in three divisions stationed at Kingston, Prescott and one constantly stationed at Gananoque "to cruize about the Islands." All bateaux leaving Prescott were to be escorted by gunboats.[145]

At Prescott, Pearson who was back in command had sent Captain Gilkison under a flag of truce in August to gain political information from his friend David Parish who had just returned from Washington. Parish presented a letter to be sent to Prevost asking that his ironworks to be immune from attack as it was "for country work only". This ironworks employed a number of deserters from Prescott. With a leading merchant in Montreal endorsing Parish, Prevost ordered that Parish's ironworks was to be left alone.[146]

Shortly after informing Prevost of 60 privateers operating out of Sackets on the St. Lawrence River on August 9, Pearson set out to find them. With a detachment of troops from the 100th Foot as well other troops garrisoned at Prescott, Pearson left the town and headed upriver to Elliott's Point, located about 5 miles above Brockville. Here he was joined by gunboats from Kingston. The following morning, Pearson's command entered Goose Creek. They throughly examined the area, but found no sign of the Americans, except where they buried their dead in a large hole. Pearson reported that "from appearances they must have been numerous." They then proceeded to "scour the Islands" but found no sign of American privateers. Before Pearson left Goose Creek two soldiers from the 100th deserted.[147]

Dissatisfied with the turn of events in the Niagara region, the Secretary of War upon orders from the President requested that Major-General Dearborn, commander of the Northern Department retire in early July. He was replaced by another Revolutionary War veteran, Major-General James Wilkinson. During the Revolution Wilkinson was involved in the conspiracy to replace George Washington. In late 1783, Wilkinson moved to Kentucky and by 1787 was involved in trade on the Mississippi. It was in that year that he began his connection with the Spanish, from whom he not only traded with, but also offered to play a role in helping Kentucky and other western communities secede from the new republic and form a connection with Spain, who controlled the port of New Orleans. For his services the Spanish would provide him with a pension for eight years starting in 1792. More intrigue would surround Wilkinson. In 1804, Wilkinson who had been back in the army for sometime, was involved in Aaron Burr's conspiracy to form a separate republic out of Louisiana and as much of Texas as they could capture. When the plan was finally exposed three years later, Wilkinson served as chief witness against Burr and was nearly indicted himself. Wilkinson weathered a congressional inquiry himself the following year. In early 1809 Wilkinson took command of the New Orleans, now part of the United States.[148]

At the start of the War of 1812, Wilkinson was still in New Orleans where he was intensely disliked. Thanks to pressure from Louisiana senators, Wilkinson received orders to head north and join Dearborn where he would serve as his chief of staff. On May 19, Wilkinson left for Washington where he arrived on July 31 and found he was to replace Dearborn.[149]

Armstrong explained to the new commander his plans for the remainder of 1813, which favored an attack on Kingston. On August 8, Armstrong wrote to Wilkinson telling him that the capture of Kingston both "on grounds of policy as of military principle, presents the first and great object of the campaign." He went onto inform the new commander that there were two ways to capture Kingston - either by "a direct or an indirect attack; by breaking down the enemy's battalion and forcing his works, or by seizing and obstructing the line of communication . . . ." The direct assault would "be the shorter and better way; but if on the contrary our strength be inferior or hardly equal to that of the enemy, the indirect attack must be preferred."

Armstrong recommended that if he was leading the expedition he would gather his force at the head of the St. Lawrence and make a demonstration of attacking Kingston, while quickly proceeding down river seizing "the northern bank at the village of Hamilton." Here he would leave troops "to fortify and hold it" while the main force continued onto Montreal where it would join the roughly 3,800 soldiers under the command of Major General Wade Hampton heading north from Lake Champlain. "In this plan," continued Armstrong, "the navy would preform its part by occupying the mouth of the river and preventing a pursuit by water, by clearing the river of the armed boats of the enemy, by holding with its own the passage at Hamilton and by giving support to that position."

If the enemy pursued the American force, stated Armstrong, they would have to travel by land with only the subsistence they could carry on their back and without artillery. If the British chose to remain stationary "his situation must soon become even more serious, as the country in which he is cannot long subsist him." The British would have no choice but to either fight their way to Quebec and "perish in the attempt" or to surrender. Armstrong finally added: "After this exposition it is unnecessary to add that in your conducting the present campaign you will make Kingston your primary object, and you will choose (as circumstances may warrant) between a direct or indirect attack upon that post."[150]

If the indirect attack was attempted, which meant attacking Montreal, Wilkinson would have to work together with Hampton and that was a problem since both men despised each other. Hampton had already informed Armstrong he will only take orders through him, not Wilkinson who was his superior.

Over two weeks later on August 26, Wilkinson was at Sackets Harbor discussing the campaign against Kingston with his senior officers, which included Major-General Morgan Lewis who was Wilkinson's second in command, Brigadier General Robert Swartout, Commodore Chauncey and Brigadier General Brown now in the regular army since July 19. Wilkinson asked the officers their opinion on four points. Should they wait in their current position to see whether the British or American squadron took control of Lake Ontario. The second option was to have a sufficient force assemble at Fort George "to cut up the enemy in that quarter," then rendezvous at Sackets with Hampton's force and move directly against Kingston. Thirdly, to have Hampton make a feint against Montreal, or take it if it seemed likely, while the troops assembled at Sackets would "reduce Kingston" and then if the season permit to move against Montreal. Finally the fourth option was in cooperation with the navy, make a feint against Kingston, then move down the St. Lawrence and join with Hampton on an attack on Montreal.

The council decided the fourth option was the best and seemed feasible. If successful, "the upper country must fall." They did add that a feint on Kingston would be "reserved for further consideration."[151]

Before he left for Fort George to personally oversee the transfer of troops to Sackets, Wilkinson left Brown instructions on his task of making preparations for the coming campaign. Brown was to have the troops, light artillery, battering guns, entrenching tools, camp equipment and baggage organized and ready to go at a day's notice by September 22. Brown was to "have a sufficient quantity of medicine, hospital stores and furniture for 10,000 men during the months of October, November and December, ready for embarkation at the same time." Twelve boats armed "with a 4, 6, or 12 pounder each, to row 30 oars and to be manned by 50 men." Brown was also to engage 300 to 400 pilots and watermen for the St. Lawrence River. Many of these men were Canadian, including William Johnston.

The son of a Loyalist from Jessup's Corps, Johnston grew up in Ernestown Township were he learned how to blacksmith and built boats. He operated a freighting business before opening a store in Kingston. In 1810 he married an American woman, which Johnston would later say was the source of his trouble. At the start of the war, Johnston served in the 1st Regiment of Frontenac Militia. In 1813 things changed when Johnston was suspected of working for the Americans and imprisoned. Johnston denied the charge, but after he escaped he did then join the American forces.[152] In the coming campaign he would pilot Wilkinson's personal boat.

Brown was also ordered to dispatch a company of men to scout along the St. Lawrence River all the way down to Ogdensburg. These men were to "repress the predatory incursions of the enemy, to watch his movements . . . and if possible to cut off intercourse with him." These troops were to conceal themselves "as much as possible from the disaffected". They were also to report to Brown "every observation and occurrence worthy of note", but they were not to cross to the Canadian side of the river "or commit any depredation on either side."[153]

On September 5, Armstrong arrived a Sackets Harbor to co-ordinate communications between Wilkinson and Hampton. Wilkinson by that time was at Fort George where he contracted "Lake fever" which put him in bed for almost two weeks. Sickness would plague Wilkinson for the upcoming campaign. It was also there that Wilkinson brought up the possibility of renewing operations on the Niagara Peninsula against the large British force there.[154]

Armstrong wrote Wilkinson on September 22 advising that if British troops investing Fort George numbered around 3,000, not counting militia and Indians, the garrison at Kingston would only number 1,200. According to Brown the garrison there were "broken down by service or intemperance." Kingston was also vulnerable due to the fact that the British fleet on Lake Ontario were aiding the troops on the Niagara Peninsula. If Kingston was captured Armstrong reminded Wilkinson, "the whole of the Upper Province westward of the mouth of the St. Lawrence, with all the British forces it contains, naval or military, falls with it." Any victory on the Niagara Peninsula would pale in comparison with the capture of Kingston.[155]

The transfer of troops to Sackets was proving difficult due to the weather. On September 25, 1,500 men were delayed from sailing for Sackets Harbor due to a strong easterly wind. Bad weather and rough water made what was normally a thirty hour trip between Fort George and Sackets Harbor much longer. The bulk of troops left on October 1 headed for Henderson Bay, southwest of Sackets, but bad weather prolonged their journey and scattered their boats. Major General Morgan Lewis writing to his wife on October 3 mentioned that troops that had left Fort George on September 27 still had not arrived yet. Lewis who had been on leave, resumed command of Sackets from Brown. While in command of the American naval post, Brown had done an excellent job in gathering supplies, provisions and anything else needed for the coming campaign.[156]

Wilkinson was in bad shape when he returned to Sackets Harbor on October 3 and had to be carried ashore. Brigadier General John Boyd, who's troops were being transferred from Fort George, said of his commander that he "was so much indisposed in mind and body that in any other service he would have perhaps been superseded in his command." Wilkinson would later state that he asked to be replaced, but Armstrong refused stating there was no one to take his place.[157]

Once at Sackets, Wilkinson made it known that he preferred making an attempt against Montreal, while simply bypassing Kingston fearing an attack against the British naval post might take longer than expected. Armstrong disagreed believing Kingston should be captured. This indecision was not a promising start to a late season campaign.[158]

Wilkinson wrote to Chauncey on October 9 asking if he could position his squadron below Kingston to keep Yeo in check "and secure a safe landing of our army in that quarter." If that was impractical, Wilkinson then asked the commodore if he could block Yeo, allowing a landing of "the army above Kingston."If these objects were abandoned, then Wilkinson would need Chauncey "to descend the ship channel and take a position to give safe passage to the army down the St. Lawrence." Chauncey replied he could secure a landing above Kingston or a safe passage down the St. Lawrence.[159]

Wilkinson's army which numbered over 7,300 men was organized into four brigades and a reserve. The First Brigade under the command of Brigadier General Boyd consisted of 5th, 13th and 12th Regiments. Boyd had joined the U.S. Army in 1786 but resigned three years later and became a soldier of fortune seeing service in India only to rejoin the U.S. Army in 1808. Brown commanded the Second Brigade which was made up of the 6th, 22nd and 15th Regiments. The Third Brigade composed of the 9th, 25th and 16th Regiments was under the command of Brigadier-General Leonard Covington, a veteran of Anthony Wayne's Indian campaign in the first half of the 1790s. Brigadier-General Robert Swartout, a former militia officer before being commissioned in the regulars, commanded the Fourth Brigade which was comprised of the 11th, 21st and 14th Regiments. The Reserve Brigade composed of the 3rd U.S. Artillery serving as infantry, the 20th Regiment, 1st U.S. Rifle Regiment and the Albany Volunteers was under the command of Colonel Alexander Macomb. The 1st and 2nd U.S. Light Dragoons were also part of the campaign. Brigadier General Moses Porter commanded the artillery.[160]

On October 16, elements of Wilkinson's force moved out by water for Grenadier Island located near the mouth of the St. Lawrence River about 18 miles from Sackets Harbor. Escorting the boats and converted merchant ships was the American squadron. The journey to Grenadier Island was horrific. The weather quickly turned bad again and stayed bad for the next two weeks. Boats crashed against the shore or were swamped sending them and their cargo to the bottom of the lake. Some troops found themselves marooned and had to be rescued. Shockingly a third or more of the army's rations were lost or ruined.[161]

Wilkinson writing on October 18 to Armstrong now seems to have changed his mind and thought that Kingston should be "the first objects of our operations." Hampton should have his orders changed, advised Wilkinson, and march his force to Morrisville. "The diminution" of his "forces by disease and various casualties" seemed to be the reason for Wilkinson's about face on the campaign's object.[162]

Armstrong also had changed his mind and now thought it unwise to make an attempt against Kingston as he believed that the British naval base had been reinforced by 1,500 troops and that Yeo's fleet was back in port there. Hampton orders would not be changed as Armstrong stated it was too late in the season to march his force from Chateauguay over a hundred miles to Morrisville on bad roads. Montreal should be the object as the Secretary of War said it was weaker than Kingston. The capture of Montreal not only would shut the St. Lawrence River to the British, but also the Ottawa River as well. Armstrong in his letter to Wilkinson added that he was open to hearing the "other side of the question" of attacking Kingston, but believe Montreal should be attacked which had "the approbation of the President" and "the sanction of a Council of War." It would seem Armstrong was having doubts about the whole campaign as he, without informing Wilkinson, issued orders for winter quarters to be constructed to hold 10,000 men about 60 or 80 miles above Montreal. Apparently Armstrong didn't believe Montreal could be reached in the remainder of the season.[163]

Wilkinson in reply to Armstrong thought that Prescott would cause trouble for an assent on Montreal. It would take time to take Prescott and with the lateness of the season, time could not be spared. Wilkinson also wanted Armstrong to direct the operations of his army against Montreal. Armstrong reminded Wilkinson that the attack on Kingston was to be either direct or indirect, especially if Kingston was reinforced as it was now. Montreal than was indirect way of taking Kingston and in a letter to Wilkinson on the 20th, Armstrong stated that he would not "change the ground of these instructions". Armstrong then left Sackets Harbor with intentions of heading to Ogdensburg, but illness prevented him from getting there.[164]

The weather on Grenadier Island where the army was rendezvousing was not improving. An officer writing about conditions on the island on October 26 said that they were "pelted daily with inexhaustible rains". He went onto say: "We have indeed for nearly a month been exposed to such torrents . . . . In consequence of the bad weather our troops from Fort George to Sackett's Harbour have been scattered everywhere along the coast . . . but most of them have now arrived here."[165] The following day the rain turned to snow and when it finished on the 28th, the island was draped in ten inches of the white stuff.

Chauncey was not happy to discover when he visited Wilkinson at Grenadier Island on October 29 that Montreal, not Kingston was to be the objective of the campaign. In a letter to the Secretary of the Navy, the commodore spelled out his reasons why Kingston should be taken first and his fears the British fleet would burn Sackets Harbor while his fleet was on the St. Lawrence. He also feared the possibility that the enemy troops, which he thought numbered 4 to 5,000 men, might cross the ice after January and burn the fleet and stores at Sackets. Nevertheless, Chauncey stated he would do his duty "to afford to the army every facility of transport and protection" in his power. He would "accompany and protect" Wilkinson's army "until it passes a point beyond which it will be perfectly secure from annoyance by the enemy's fleet." Then he would get out of the St. Lawrence before he was trapped by ice.[166]

The expedition got underway on October 31, when Brown left Grenadier Island with his Second Brigade bound for French Creek 25 miles away. The rest of the army was to leave the following day, but bad weather flared up again postponing the departure for two days. Despite its stalls and starts, the campaign for Montreal was on.

CHAPTER 7
FAILURE AT CHATEAUGUAY
1813

If the Americans were unsure of their point of attack for so long, the British were as equally confused. On October 12, Pearson writing to Baynes from Prescott had received information that the Americans had 6,000 troops and 300 boats at Sackets Harbor under Wilkinson and were going to attack either Montreal or Prescott, but not Kingston. Hampton's force was "reduced by Desertion to 5000". Pearson also reported 400 U.S. Dragoons "carelessly posted at Malone" which might be cut off. The dragoons moving by land from Sackets Harbor were "20 to 30 Miles on their route Eastward."[167]

Colonel Nelson Luckett with his 1st Regiment of United States Dragoons arrived at Ogdensburg on October 11. Luckett was to examine the country in advance of Wilkinson's army. The following day, court was being held in Ogdensburg when artillery fire was heard across the river from Prescott. Court was adjourned and just in time as a 24 pound shot smashed in a room above the court house where the grand jury had been meeting. Luckett withdrew from town.[168] Pearson, having received information that some of Luckett's "picquets was stationed at a large mill about eight miles from Prescott" was determined to capture them. The task was given to Major Cockburn and a detachment of the Canadian Fencibles, which managed to capture or destroy the whole party, except for two troopers who escaped. The prisoners were to be sent down river to Montreal.

With no move being made against St. Regis by Hampton's army, Pearson sent Major James Dennis with the flank companies of the 49th Foot to Cornwall. The Voltigeurs, Pearson kept at Johnstown located not far from Prescott, in case they were needed. Pearson believed the Americans would make an attempt against Kingston or

Prescott and was waiting for a message from Sackets which he expected that night.[169]

A spy[170] had crossed the river above Prescott with the purpose of gathering information on the Americans. Once across the river he went to the Quaker settlement south of Ogdensburg. From there he "sent on trusty friends" who went to Sackets Harbor where they reported a large force of "6,000 regulars and 1,000 volunteers from the militia, intended for an expedition to Canada." The "trusty friends" also reported that the American force gathering there "had 150 large boats, 17 gunboats and 17 scows for artillery, horses and forage." Although Prescott was rumoured to be the destination of this large force, this was only a ruse to draw off troops from Kingston, which was the real intent for the American expedition. All this information was delivered to Kingston on October 17.[171]

De Rottenburg after receiving information "through the medium of a respectable inhabitant [Samuel Casey] who was sent by Colonel Cartwright" on the American built up at Sackets, sent a message to Prevost on the 18th. The Polish born British general speculated that the enemy was frustrated in their designs against Kingston "by the rapid movement of [British] troops and of the squadron" there meant to "establish himself at York". De Rottenburg believed the American never had any serious intentions against Prescott or Lower Canada. Three days earlier, however he had wrote to Prevost reporting on the Americans assembling a large flotilla at Sackets and the rumor among their seamen was that Kingston was their objective. By October 30, De Rottenburg now believed Kingston was going to be attacked as did Yeo.[172]

Reports of a severe defeat of the British Right Division in western Upper Canada on October 5 at Moraviantown by an American force under Major General William Harrison caused alarm among the British and Canadian troops in the Niagara Peninsula. With western Upper Canada under American control, Harrison was in a position to push east and cut off the British Centre Division. To prevent this, the British commander, Major General Vincent, withdrew his troops to Burlington Bay. De Rottenberg gave him the choice to fall back to York if need be. Eventually the situation stabilized when it was discovered that Harrison was not pushing east.

With the collapse of the British Right Division, the Centre Division became the Right Division which encompassed the area west of Kingston, while Kingston "and the Troops to the Eastward in the Upper Province" now became the Centre Division. While "all Troops from Coteau du Lac West of Quebec" were now the Left Division.[173]

    Lieutenant Colonel 'Red George' Macdonell, who had been transferred from Prescott to Kingston in June and was in command of the 1st Light Battalion of Select Embodied Militia of Lower Canada, received orders on October 20 to head to Lower Canada. The following day, Macdonell set off down the St. Lawrence River with his men reaching the south shore of St. Lawrence at Beauharnois late on the 24th. From there they marched 20 miles to the Chateauguay River. It was here that Hampton's army had pushed into Lower Canada as part of the second prong of the American campaign against Montreal.

    Hampton had originally crossed the border into Lower Canada on September 19, pushing to around Odletown. Due to a hot, dry summer Hampton discovered that many of the streams and wells in the area were dried up. After a council of war with his officers, Hampton ordered his army to withdraw back into New York and march west to the Chateauguay River where his army would be better supplied by water.

    On October 16, Armstrong wrote to Hampton of Wilkinson's coming "descent of the St. Lawrence" and ordered him to move to "the mouth of Chateauguay" or some other point which would "favour our junction, and hold the enemy in check."[174] Five days later Hampton crossed his army of roughly 4,000 troops, many of whom were recruits and poorly disciplined, 200 dragoons and 10 artillery pieces across the border. The following day, the advance guard had penetrated to within 15 miles of where the Chateauguay River flows into the St. Lawrence. The advance was slowed down somewhat as it took two days for the rest of the army to catch up. The New York militia, 1,400 men in all, refused to march into Lower Canada. This was not an uncommon action for American militia during the war.

    Blocking the American advance where the Chateauguay took a sharp turn was a smaller Lower Canadian force under the command of Lieutenant Colonel Charles-Michel d'Irumberry de Salaberry. He had around 300 men from his unit - the Voltigeurs, as well the Canadian Fencibles and Sedentary Militia, plus about 20 Abenaki

Indians as his first line of defence. The Voltigeurs were deployed as skirmishers, while the militia continued work on an abatis.[175] About a mile behind them were four more lines of defence protected by breastworks that Salaberry had set up about 200 yards apart, while the fourth was about half a mile back. This line guarded a ford to the east side of the river.

In all there were about 1,800 troops, the bulk of them French Canadian, to hold these defences. Overall command was under Major General Louis de Watteville, a Swiss officer who commanded a regiment of Swiss and other foreign soldiers in the British service. This was only the outer crust in Prevost's plan to defend Montreal. Prevost, believing the American meant to take Montreal, set about protecting the city. He had about 5,500 regulars, fencibles and embodied militia and about 8,000 sedentary militia of which roughly a quarter were armed while the rest played support roles in the moving of supplies. While de Watteville's command took up position along the Chateauguay, a second force acted as reserve between them and Montreal under the command of Major General Sheaffe.[176]

Being informed of the defences that faced him, Hampton ordered 1,500 men under the command of Colonel Robert Purdy to move out under the cover of darkness along the right side of the river and capture the ford putting them in the rear of the Lower Canadians. While Purdy moved into position, another force under the command of Brigadier General George Izard was to make a frontal assault against the main position the following day.

Led by guides, who as it turned out knew little of the ten miles of swampy, thick country they had to pass through, Purdy's men set out late in the day of October 25. By daylight of the following morning they had not reached their objectives when Izard moved out. Izard's force came under fire from the small number of troops holding the abatis. Halting his men, Izard waited for the signal that Purdy was making his flank attack.

Purdy continued on toward his objective but soon his advance guard bumped into some militia and Indian pickets. The pickets gave way, but were reinforced by some of Macdonell's men which crossed the river to support them. Purdy's advance guard fell back on the main body fearing more Indians. Hampton now aware that Purdy was no where near capturing the ford, ordered him to fall back and cross the river.

At 2 P.M. Izard began his main attack. A firefight commenced between the American troops and the small force holding the abatis. Much of the American volley fire was high, while the Lower Canadian's fire was more accurate. With this firefight raging, Macdonell marched to the aid of Salaberry. 'Red George' was joined by a group of Indians, which he immediately sent to threaten Izard's left flank with gunfire and war-whoops. A dozen buglers also went with them to sound 'the advance' while his men shouted loudly.

Purdy attempting to withdraw, so as to be able to cross the river, meanwhile, was attacked by the detachment Macdonell had sent over along with the militia already posted there amounting to around 80 men. They caused confusion in Purdy's ranks, but the Americans managed to rally and beat off the Lower Canadians. A second attack by the Lower Canadians fared little better and Purdy continued his withdraw.

Seeing that the main attack had failed, Hampton ordered Izard to withdraw. The Americans had suffered about 50 casualties while the Lower Canadians had 5 killed and 16 wounded. Hampton ordered a retreat across the border. On November 1 he wrote to Armstrong informing him that he considered the campaign ended. He also informed the Secretary of War that he intended to resign after the troops were put into winter quarters.[177]

Smaller actions took place on the St. Lawrence River in late October as a brigade of 12 bateaux were headed upriver from Cornwall under escort. Reaching the head of the Rapid du Plat, the brigade halted for the night. Privateer Benjamin Richards from Hamilton, New York with a volunteer party of citizens slipped across the river sometime before morning and captured the bateaux and its crews. Some of the captured goods where taken to a warehouse in Hamilton, while some of the lighter goods were taken to Madrid.[178]

Another brigade of bateaux, this time numbering 36 headed upriver. Besides the ten or twelve regulars guarding the boats, a strong escort of the 1st Company, 2nd Regiment of Glengarry Militia under Captain Alex McMillan and Captain George Merkley with 120 Dundas militia were added to protect the brigade from capture.

At the foot of Rapid du Plat, the brigade stopped for the night. Early the following morning, Americans were spotting in force on Ogden's Island, apparently preparing to attack. Despite this the bateaux were pulled up through the rapids. Meanwhile, Pearson at Prescott, upon hearing that several attempts would be made against the bateaux sent Captain Skinner with the orders that any cargo destined for Prescott was to be loaded onto wagons and taken by land, while the rest of the cargo should be returned to Cornwall. By 11 P.M. the wagons were loaded. An exaggerated report reached the militia that 500 dismounted U.S. dragoons had landed and where advancing toward them.

Merkley and McMillan decided to meet them half way. The wagons were moved away from the river and orders were left for the bateaux crews to take their boats to Hoople Creek once gunfire was heard. They were to wait there for the escort to return. The two militia officers now took their men towards Mariatown. The roads were muddy and in rough condition as the militiamen moved on through the cold night. Moonlight soon revealed a large party heading toward them. This party was recognized as American dragoons by their white trousers and white horsehair that were on their helmets. The Dundas and Glengarry men immediately set up an ambush and when the American dragoons were within pistol shot away they fired upon them causing 11 casualties. Unable to see their enemy, the Americans quickly fled with the militia in pursuit. With reports of more Americans landing upriver, the militia was called off the chase. Meanwhile, the U.S. dragoons reached their boats and quickly headed for the other side of the river. By 2 A.M., the militia was heading towards Hoople Creek, reaching the bridge that spanned it by sunrise. Finding the bateaux safe, they all headed onto Cornwall.[179]

The Kingston Gazette reported another attack on shipping on November 6. Seven boats containing private property, the paper said, were headed upriver from Montreal for Kingston when they were captured sometime the previous week about 12 miles below Prescott.[180] These little skirmishes were nothing to the fighting that lay just ahead.

CHAPTER 8
CRYSLER'S FARM
1813

On the last day of October, Brown's 2nd Brigade left Grenadier Island. They moved down the St. Lawrence River to French Creek where they stopped for the night. To protect his camp, Brown had a detachment of artillery positioned on a rocky point on the west side of the mouth of French Creek. Bad weather prevented the rest of the army from leaving Grenadier Island to join Brown. The weather did not stop the Royal Navy however.

Captain William Mulcaster RN, with a small armada consisting of the *Lord Melville*, *Earl of Moira*, *Sir Sidney Smith*, *Beresford* and four gunboats pushed through the snowstorm towards French Creek. Upon passing the rocky point on November 1, Mulcaster's vessels took enemy musket and artillery fire. They returned the greeting with grape and cannister fire which forced the Americans off the point.

Once Mulcaster rounded the point, he found Brown's troops formed in "three columns with a battery of two brass 18-pounders in front and a numerous train of artillery on their flanks." Mulcaster managed to squeeze three of his warships into the bay at the creek's mouth. For almost an hour both sides exchanged fire. Captain Francis Spilsbury RN commanding the gunboats, pulled along the eastern bank and "kept up an animated fire" on the Americans. With daylight fading accurate fire became hindered with the American troops becoming hard to spot among the trees. This along with the fact that his vessels had taken some hits, Mulcaster decided "to haul off for the night."

A strong wind kept the gunboats from moving during the night to annoy Brown's force. By daylight the next morning, the wind had let off allowing Mulcaster to attack again. Brown had a surprise awaiting him. During the night, the Americans mounted some guns and had constructed a furnace enabling them to fire red hot shot. Spotting the American bateaux and scows on shore and deciding it would cost to many lives to try and destroy them, Mulcaster headed back to Kingston with 1 killed and 6 wounded. The Americans had suffered 10 casualties.[181]

"After many delays and losses by incessant storms we have at length succeeded in getting the whole of army, except the rearguard, safe into the St. Lawrence," wrote Lewis to his wife on November 2. He mentioned that he and Wilkinson, who was very feeble, would join the rearguard the next day. He predicted that once their army joined with Hampton, they would place their "standard even on the walls of Quebec." Writing to Armstrong on the 3rd, Wilkinson requested that the Secretary of War "notify Hampton of the point of junction". According to Wilkinson, Hampton had treated his "authority with contempt" and would act only on orders from Armstrong.[182]

That same day Wilkinson arrived at French Creek and learned of the battle. With his illness getting worse, the American commander had to be carried on shore. Wilkinson was not the only one who was sick. A good portion of his army was ill as well. Nevertheless the campaign continued.[183]

With the weather improving on November 4, the day was spent organizing the flotilla. At 5 A.M. the next morning, an hour after the troops had been up, the signal gun boomed for the flotilla to get underway. The weather was pleasant as the flotilla passed through the Thousand Islands. Wilkinson's army stopped for the night near Morrisville. Knowing that his flotilla had been spotted by enemy's gunboats and a gig, Wilkinson planned to pass Prescott during the night, but due to the confusion during the trip down river the order was countermanded.[184]

While the army moved down river, Chauncey faced Yeo who brought his squadron to within five miles of the American fleet on the north side of Wolfe Island and anchored off Grindstone Island. A chain of small islands, joined by rocks and reefs separated the opposing fleets. There was only one passage near the foot of Wolfe Island which could take vessels drawing less than 12 feet of water to get them into the North Channel where Yeo was. On the 6th, Chauncey sent boats to sound out this passage so as to be able to get his ships through to face the British. No battle would rage though, as Yeo withdrew to Kingston. Fearing the British would mount some guns at Carleton Island trapping him in the river, Chauncey moved his fleet to the island and then onto Gravelly Point and eventually to Sackets Harbor where he arrived on November 11.[185]

On November 6, Wilkinson's flotilla pushed to within three miles of Ogdensburg. Feeling a little better, Wilkinson reconnoitered Prescott in his gig. Meanwhile the powder and fixed ammunition was unloaded from the boats and put in carts to be moved by land during the night. When Wilkinson returned he ordered the bulk of the soldiers to disembark. They like the powder and ammunition would travel by land during the cover of darkness to avoid the British guns at Prescott. The boats would be slipped past Prescott at night with only skeleton crews under Brown.[186]

It was here that Wilkinson issued a proclamation to the Upper Canada inhabitants on the north side of the river:

"The Army of the United States which I have the honour to command, invades this Province to conquer, and not to destroy; to subdue the forces of His Britanic Majesty, and not to war against its unoffending Subjects - Those therefore among you, who remain quiet at home, should Victory incline to the American Standard, shall be protected in their persons and property -

But those who are found in Arms must necessarily be treated as avowed enemies -

To menace is unmanly - To seduce dishonorable - Yet it is just and humane to place these alternatives before you."[187]

At noon on the same day, Colonel William King, adjutant-general of Hampton's army, arrived with a dispatch from that general intended for Armstrong. King had gone to Sackets Harbor to find the Secretary of War, but not finding him thought it proper to find out if Wilkinson had any communication for Hampton. Wilkinson had King take a letter to Hampton telling him he intended to attack Montreal "if not prevented by some act of God". He told Hampton that "the division under your command must cooperate with the corps under my immediate orders" and that a junction be made between the two armies. Wilkinson told Hampton "that your own judgement should determine the point". After gaining a foothold on

Montreal Island, Wilkinson boasted that they would take the city or end up in "honourable graves." Wilkinson also told Hampton that he had only 15 days of bread left for his army and 20 days worth of meat. He wished Hampton to forward two or three months of supplies that were stored in magazines at Lake Champlain. Finally Wilkinson expected to see or hear from Hampton at St. Regis by the 9th.[188]

On November 1, Pearson had ordered Lieutenant Duncan Clark of the Incorporated Militia to take up a position at Elliot's Point, five miles upriver from Brockville to watch the river. Pearson's orders were direct: "You will upon the appearance of an enemy, instantly take horse, and repair to Prescott, with all possible diligence, alarming the country as you pass down." Four days later Clark spotted Wilkinson's flotilla of 300 vessels of various description as well as gunboats. Taking the first horse he could find from a local farmer, Clark rode toward Prescott spreading the alarm as he went. The troops there prepared for action.[189]

Another officer send out by Pearson was Captain Richard Duncan Fraser, who along with Assistant Barracks Master William Fitzpatrick and a few dragoons were ordered to scout out the enemy and order any militiaman they saw to Prescott. Riding into Brockville on the night of November 6, Fraser bumped into Adjutant Hiram Spafford. Fraser would later report that he asked why Spafford was not at Prescott, which the Adjutant responded that he was looking after his property instead. Fraser ordered him arrested, but Spafford escaped. Fraser headed for the man's house, forced the door open and searched the house for Spafford but was unable to find him. Spafford's servant would later testify that both Fraser and Fitzpatrick were drunk and after searching the house, attempted to set it on fire. Spafford later sued Fraser for breaking his lock and false imprisonment. At the civil trial it was reported that Fraser had acted "most violent and brutal" and was found guilty. It was also made known that Spafford had not escaped, but rather had been allowed to get his horse, but when he did not return as quick as Fraser would have liked, the dragoon Captain went to his home and busted in. Spafford was awarded over £49 for his trouble.[190]

A fog rolled in around 8 P.M. on that same night Fraser rode into Brockville. Wilkinson down river at Ogdensburg gave his troops the order to march overland, while the boats set off with muffled oars. Getting into his gig, followed by his family in his passage-boat, Wilkinson led the way. A "sudden change of the atmosphere" exposed his passage-boat to the guns at Prescott. The vessel came under heavy fire, as did the troops moving by land who were spotted by the "gleam of their arms". Brown, in charge of getting the boats past Prescott, ordered the flotilla to halt until the moon had set.

The boats were spotted again as the American flotilla moved out a second time. This time the boats didn't stop. For three hours the guns at Prescott fired on the American boats but to little effect. Only 1 man was killed and 2 wounded. By 10 A.M. on November 7, all the vessels except for two, rendezvoused below Prescott. The two vessels, loaded with provisions, artillery and ordnance stores were grounded near Ogdensburg. They came under fire and it took the Americans nearly half the day to get them free.[191]

At Red Mills the troops climbed back into the boats and started down river again. When they reached Johnstown, the Americans spotted some Canadian militia, along with a couple of Royal Artillery guns. Fearing the enemy side of the river would be "lined with posts of musketry and artillery at every narrow pass of the river", Macomb's Elite Corps with 1,200 men was ordered at 1 P.M. to clear "these obstructions."[192]

After passing through the Galop Rapids, Macomb's men reached Iroquois Point. Here the river was especially narrow, only about 500 yards wide. Posted on the Point was a militia picket of a dozen men of the 1st Dundas Regiment of Militia. The men fired on the Americans. Two hundred Dundas militiamen posted in a hollow nearby under the command of Captain John Munroe rushed to join the pickets and fired on the Americans as well.

The Americans quickly landed their boats on the opposite side of the river, but not for long. Macomb's troops crossed the river landing near Jacob Brouse's farm, who happen to be one of the pickets firing on the Americans. Munroe's men quickly took to the woods, knowing they could not stop the Americans.[193] Major Forsyth, who's riflemen were part of the Elite Corps, landed further upriver.

The main American force set out about 3:30 P.M.. After passing through the Galop Rapids, they took fire from British guns.

Lieutenant Colonel Abram Eustis moved his gun barges in close to the British guns "and a cannonade ensued without injury to either side." Meanwhile, Forsyth advanced his riflemen towards the enemy guns. They came upon some vedettes, who galloped off and quickly warned the Royal artillerymen. The bluecoated artillerymen promptly limbered up their guns and pulled out before Forsyth reached them.[194]

The flotilla did not push much further before stopping for the night. Macomb continued to clear the north side of the river. He destroyed a blockhouse and halted for the night a mile below modern Iroquois, Ontario.[195]

The following morning, November 8, Wilkinson's flotilla moved down river till they reached the "White House" a short piece from Iroquois Point on the American side of the river. Brown's brigade was ordered to cross the river and support Macomb in clearing the enemy from north bank. Both regiments of dragoons, about 400 troopers, were crossed over the St. Lawrence River as well. The transfer took the whole day and the following night.

It was also at the "White House" that Wilkinson had a council of war with his senior officers to determine the future of the campaign. A confidential agent who left Montreal five days earlier reported that the British had 600 fortified troops with artillery at Coteau du Lac, along with another 200 troops with artillery on a nearby island. There was a similar number of troops with artillery pieces on the south shore. Roughly 200 or 300 troops were at the Cedars, while at Montreal there was reported 200 sailors, 400 marines and an unknown number of militia. There was also 2,500 regulars expected. It was discovered that there were 400 troops at Cornwall and that 60 bateaux full of troops, with armed vessels had arrived at Prescott this morning. In light of this information Wilkinson asked his officers if the army, which numbered 7,000 and was expecting another 4,000 under Hampton at St. Regis, should move as quick as possible and attack Montreal. Lewis, Boyd, Brown and Swartout believed they "should proceed to Montreal, the object of the expedition", while Covington and Porter were of the opinion "that we proceed from this place under great danger from the want of proper transport, pilots, &c., but are anxious to meet the enemy at Montreal because we know of no other alternative."[196]

Wilkinson's information that the 60 bateaux full of British troops had arrived at Prescott was accurate, but a bit premature. The day before, November 7, it started to become clearer to De Rottenberg where Wilkinson was headed when it was report that artillery had been heard firing at Prescott the night before from Gananoque. This meant the Americans must have passed the little river community on their way to Montreal.[197] De Rottenberg had earlier been ordered by Prevost to form a "corps of observation" under the command of Lieutenant-Colonel Joseph Morrison of the 89th Foot to pursue Wilkinson if he headed down river.

Described as a "most attentive, zealous, clear officer", Morrison has been born in New York City in 1783 the son of the deputy commissary general of North America. He was commissioned as ensign in the 83rd Foot ten years later. The following year he became a lieutenant. Active service for Morrison did not begin until 1799, and he was to see some action in the Netherlands where he was wounded. For the next 14 years Morrison would see little combat, doing mostly garrison duty before arriving in British North America in 1812.[198]

An officer who had did have combat experience was Lieutenant Colonel John Harvey, who served as Morrison second in command. Born in England, Harvey had joined the army in 1794 as an ensign. He was to see active duty in the Netherlands, the coast of France, Cape of Good Hope, Ceylon, Egypt and India. After a stint in Ireland he was sent to Upper Canada where he served as deputy adjutant general to Vincent. After having scouted out the enemy, Harvey led the night attack against the Americans at Stoney Creek in June of 1813.[199]

The "corps of observation" Morrison commanded consisted of eight companies of the 49th Foot, which due to casualties and sickness from hard fighting in the Niagara region numbered about 160 men. This unit was under the command of Lieutenant Colonel Charles Plenderleath. Also part of Morrison's small force was the 2nd Battalion of the 89th Foot which numbered about 450 men. There was also a small detachment of Royal Artillery personnel with two 6-pounder guns. About midmorning on the 7th, Morrison "corps of observation" embarked in about 60 bateaux, escorted by two schooners *Lord Beresford* and *Sir Sidney Smith*, along with seven gunboats under the command of Mulcaster and set off for Prescott. They did not reach Prescott until the evening of the 8th.[200]

The following morning they set out early in pursuit of

Wilkinson. Morrison's little force had grown as he was reinforced with Pearson and part of the Prescott garrison. Pearson's force consisted of three 6-pounders, three companies of Canadian Voltigeurs, two companies of Canadian Fencibles, along with the two flank companies of the 49th and thirty Mohawks from Tyendinaga located along the Bay of Quinte. Ahead on the King's Highway which follows the river, were a handful of troopers from Fraser's Provincial Light Dragoons. Morrison force now numbered about 800 men.[201] At Prescott, Morrison was forced to leave behind two schooners which drew too much water to make it through the rapids up ahead. Mulcaster's gunboats continued on though.

A brief skirmish broke out between Forsyth's 1st U.S. Rifle Regiment and the Mohawks and Canadian militia not long after Morrison's force came ashore just above Iroquois Point. The Americans had one man killed before driving off the militia and Mohawks. The U.S. dragoons, with four light artillery pieces, along with Brown's command marched out on the King's Highway with orders to clear the north bank all the way to the Long Sault Rapids. The flotilla moved out as well, but had to hold up and wait for several hours to allow Brown's troops to keep up. Morrison's much smaller force threatened the American's rear but made no serious attack against it. About 5 P.M., Wilkinson's army stopped for the night at the "Yellow House" having traveled about 11 miles that day.[202]

This house belonged to Captain John Crysler of the 1st Dundas Regiment of Militia. Crysler like many inhabitants along the north bank of the upper St. Lawrence River was a Loyalist. He had been born in Schoharie, New York in 1770. During the American Revolution he served a drummer in the hard hitting Butler's Rangers. After the war he settled with his father in Williamsburg Township. After receiving a tavern license in 1801, Crysler began importing liquor, salt and tobacco in from Lower Canada. Three years later he was elected to the House of Assembly and in 1806 was appointed the justice of peace for the Eastern District. At the same time, Crysler began to purchase large amounts of land in the Finch and Mountain townships that were rich in timber.[203]

The next day, November 10, Morrison along with Mulcaster stopped at Hamilton with a small force and demanded the surrender of goods, mostly belonging to merchants at Kingston, captured in late

October by Benjamin Richards at Rapid du Plat. Morrison's troops were in the process of gathering up the goods, when cannon fire was heard down river. Impatient to be going, Morrison had a 6-pounder artillery piece found in the village spiked and ordered that the goods and the buildings they were stored in to be torched. Fearing that the fire might spread to the rest of the village, Hamilton's leading citizens begged Morrison not to do this. They agreed instead to deliver the goods across the river "at the House of Jacob Wager" the following day. Some barracks in the town were set still ablaze.[204]

The British and Canadian troops continued their pursuit of Wilkinson. Upon reaching the house of John Parlow, an officer asked how long it had been since the Americans passed his place. Parlow told him: "You needn't follow them for they are ten to your one." The officer retorted: "Never mind that, my man, we are not asking your opinion."[205]

Further down river the same day, Brown received orders from Wilkinson to continue to march his command, minus two artillery pieces and the 2nd Regiment of Light Dragoons, along the north bank clearing it of enemy troops. Boyd, who was to command the remaining brigades, was to take precautions against the enemy "from making an advantageous attack; and if attacked is to turn about and beat them." With the dangerous Long Sault rapids facing them, Wilkinson ordered that all commanding officers of brigades and regiments to examine the boats to make sure they were properly fitted for the journey through the rapids.[206]

Brown's command moved out about noon and soon engaged the enemy near a blockhouse built along the rapids. About this time, Morrison's troops were spotted by the Americans moving towards their rear. A sharp little skirmish broke out in the rain, mainly between the Royal Artillery guns under Captain Henry Jackson and American infantry with neither side gaining an advantage over the other. The fighting however did not end there. Mulcaster's gunboats moved in on the American boats still at shore and opened up on them. Wilkinson ordered two 18-pounder artillery pieces to be run on shore and formed into a battery. Muclaster's gunboats pulled back after taking fire from the American battery. These little actions did little harm to Wilkinson's force, except waste valuable time for them. With darkness coming on, the river pilots refused to run the flotilla down the Long Sault Rapids. The army moved three miles east and stopped for the night at Michael Cook's tavern. Wilkinson by this time had become so sick he was unable to sit up and was confined to his bed on his passage-boat.[207]

Brown, meanwhile, after having destroyed the blockhouse continued along the King's Highway heading for Cornwall. At Hoople Creek about 11 miles west of Cornwall, Brown's men ran into resistance in the form about 400 Glengarry militia under the command of Major James Dennis of the 49th Foot. At 1 P.M., Dennis writing from a fence, quickly penned a short note to Colonel Hercules Scott at Coteau du Lac describing the situation that faced him. His militia were facing the enemy's advance at a bridge he had earlier destroyed over Hoople Creek. "They have brought up two field pieces, which obliges my retiring by the wood parallel to the Glengarry Road." Dennis intended to annoy Brown's advance when he could with his raw militia under his command who were "completely undisciplined, altho they are reluctant of retiring, and when acting with regulars will be an efficient and daring force." Dennis ordered his men back when the Americans attempted to gain his right flank.[208] Although forced to retreat, Dennis had slowed down Brown's advance who had to rebuild the bridge across Hoople Creek. Brown would not reach Cornwall on the 10th.

Cornwall was in great consternation nevertheless. The government stores at the town were loaded into a 150 wagons and rolled out for St. Andrews and then on to McMartin's Mills where they stopped for the night. Around 6 P.M., Dennis with his militia arrived there as well. Dennis had some of the supplies stored at McMartin's Mills for the use of troops posted there, while other stores were taken to "Rev. McDonald's". The rest were to be sent to Coteau du Lac. Some of the supplies were deposited on the Concession Road from Cornwall during the retreat, which Dennis thought would be plundered. In writing to Scott at Coteau on November 11, Dennis looked for supplies to be sent from there by the back roads to him. Dennis unhappily stated that since his arrival at McMartin's Mills that many of the militia had deserted to their homes. He expounded further: "The dreadful state of the roads and severe rainy weather, has tended much to excite a disposition to this criminal conduct, and the inefficiency of many old but ignorant and indolent officers to keep them under control." A Royal Marine officer, Captain Cochrane, writing from McMartin's Inn to Scott on the same day also commented on the militia officers: " . . . I am sorry to say their officers are very bad, particularly the two Colonels. The men well disposed, and, I am convinced, had they officers, would behave well."[209]

    A cold rain made the night miserable for the American troops encamped at Cook's Tavern. For the most of the campaign, the American soldiers had "behaved themselves like gentleman" as described by local farmers. The Americans paid for the stores they needed from local farmers with Spanish dollars. The American officers were courteous and laid down strict orders to their men to respect the farmer's homes and household goods. Hay and grain on the other hand seemed to be seen as lawful booty as did fence rails used for campfires. There were other exceptions as well. On the march near Rapid du Plat, some American troops had ransacked a house belonging to man named Burgoyne in search of hidden military stores. At an abandoned store owned by man named Glassford, some troops helped themselves to new boots and clothing. As well some soldiers who marched through Matilda and Williamsburg townships feasted on honey they found there. This was much to their misery, as many of them became sick with dysentery.[210]

    Morrison had moved his little army to take possession of Crysler's Farm where they camped for the night and endured the miserable weather. The British commander set up his headquarters in John Crysler's house. Crysler along with Captain Reuben Sherwood were both acting as aides to Morrison. A meeting was called by Morrison with his senior officers to determine their next move. Orders had been sent to Morrison to return to Kingston immediately as a large rumored American force was said to be forming at Gravelly Point across the river from Kingston in a position to threaten the important naval base. Despite the odds facing them, Morrison and his officers decided they would not pull back, but rather fight.[211]

    The terrain at Crysler's Farm and surrounding area was to Morrison's liking. There was a road, lined on either side by a heavy cedar log fence about 5 feet high, that led from the river for about half a mile north to the forest. This would be the western edge of the coming battle and provide good cover. The thick forest to the north was swampy and made movement for troops difficult. To the south ran the King's Highway parallel to the river. The fields that stretched to the east for quarter of mile and north for half a mile were covered with fall wheat. Past that lay ploughed ground cut by two gullies and ended with a steep bank down a large ravine. Another ravine was located in the woods east of the cleared fields. This whole area lay on plateau about 25 feet higher than the river that ran along beside it.

     The next morning, November 11, was grey and damp with a cold east wind, but a least the rain had stopped. The dragoons serving with Brown reportedly reached Cornwall about 7 A.M. Sending word back to Wilkinson that the Long Sault Rapids were clear of the enemy, Brown's main force pushed onto Cornwall where they found only women and children. When the town was reached, the officers moved into some of the farm houses, while the soldiers set up camp in the nearby fields. The American soldiers, described as not being very disciplined or drilled, behaved civil and quiet and did not insult any of occupants of the houses. They did however take what contents they needed from the barns and granaries and used the fence rails for fuel for their fires. Searches were also made for valuables concealed in the gardens or cellars. More alarming for the residents there was talk of the Americans destroying the town before pushing onto Montreal.[212]

     Back at the British and Canadian camp, picket fire caused alarm around 8 A.M.. Word quickly spread that the Americans were advancing toward them. The troops were quickly formed up ready for action. A little less then two miles away at Cook's Tavern, where the American army was encamped, a dragoon officers finally came from Brown's command around 10:30 A.M. with word that they had forced the enemy and "would reach the foot of the Saut early in the day." Wilkinson gave orders for the flotilla to get moving when Mulcaster's gunboats struck again.[213]

     Mulcaster with his gunboats, including the 60 foot *Nelson*, moved out to harass the Americans. The best position would have been mid-river so as to get the best field of fire, but the fast current made that impossible. One of the gunboats was ordered to anchor at the foot of a hundred acre island covered in maple trees located in the middle of the river opposite Crysler's farm. Another gunboat took up position directly opposite Crysler's house. The *Nelson*, meanwhile, with its 24-pounder took up position at the head of some rush-bed upriver. The British vessels opened up on the enemy, but did little damage.[214]

The very ill Wilkinson was soon informed that the enemy was moving towards him. Then came contradictory reports as well as information on the "movements and counter-movements" of the enemy gunboats. Wilkinson finally ordered Colonel Joseph Swift of the U.S. Engineers to tell Boyd to take his command of roughly 2,500 men, composing his own brigade, as well as that of Covington and Swartout in three columns and outflank the enemy if possible and take their artillery. Boyd also received reports that "about two hundred British and Indians had advanced into the woods" that skirted his rear.[215]

The reports were accurate. Morrison had earlier sent out Major Frederick Heriot with three companies of the Canadian Voltiguers, thirty Mohawks led by Lieutenant Charles Anderson of the British Indian Department and twelve troopers from Fraser's Light Provincial Dragoons as skirmishers. Heriot's skirmishers now moved through the woods west of the cleared fields toward the Americans. One of Heriot's men stopped at a house belonging to a widow and her 11 year old daughter near the woods and told them to get in the cellar as there was going to be a battle.[216]

Boyd immediately ordered Brigadier-General Swartout to take his Fourth Brigade and attack Heriot's skirmishers. Covington's Third Brigade was ordered "to be within supporting distance". About 2 P.M., Swartout "dashed into the woods and with the 21st Infantry (a part of his brigade) under the command of Colonel Eleazer Wheelock Ripley after a short skirmish drove them back . . .." The Voltigeurs and Mohawks took cover in a ravine, which they kept a sharp fire on the advancing American blue coats. They were shortly after driven from there as well.[217]

Once the Americans reached the clearing west of the woods they found that Morrison "had judiciously chosen his ground."[218] The 49th in their grey greatcoats and the 89th in their redcoats to the left of them "thrown more to the rear, with a gun, formed the main body and reserve, and extended almost from the road to woods" on the left. The Mohawks and the Voltigeurs now driven back had taken up position in this swampy thick forest. The dragoons meanwhile had galloped back to the British lines with word of the American's advance. Pearson with the flank companies of the 49th, two companies of the Canadian Fencibles and one gun was on the British right, a little advanced on the King's Highway. Captain George Barnes with three companies of the 89th, "formed in echelon" with a gun was to the left of Pearson.[219]

The Royal Artillery guns greeted the American brigades as they cleared the woods with shrapnel and roundshot. Harvey writing of the battle the following day stated that the Americans had "riflemen on his right and in his front."Major John Woodford's 2nd Regiment of U.S. Light Dragoons took up a position on the King's Highway. The two guns attached to Boyd's force had not yet arrived due to "the nature of the ground and the circuitous route they had to take . . . ."[220]

Swartout's Brigade with Boyd's First Brigade under the command of Colonel Isaac Coles, moved forward with orders to the hit the British left flank. Ripley described the advance of his regiment as "slow and hard" through "muddy fields for half a mile".[221] Most of Swarthout's troops formed in column, found it hard going through the swamps and thick forest. Harassed by skirmish fire from the Voltigeurs and Mohawks, the Americans drove them off and emerged out of the forest on the British left flank. To meet this threat Morrison ordered the 89th to refuse its left placing its "battalion at right angles to the 49th." The bulk of the American troops were still in column advancing from the forest and were hit by the 89th fire, as well as artillery fire. According to Harvey, the American's "columns halted and commenced a heavy but irregular fire, which our battalions returned with infinitely more effect by regular firing of platoons and wings." Morrison reported that the 89th and 49th moved "forward occasionally firing by platoons."[222] The American attacked was halted as the troops broke for the rear.

Ripley's 21st Regiment attempted to cover the retreat, but his men soon emptied their cartridge boxes firing at the British. "My men, disregarding my officers," later wrote Ripley, "dodged behind stumps and opened individual fire."[223] Ripley could not stop them from shooting until they ran out of ammunition and then he could not stop them from retiring. He did eventually rally his men.

With the British left flank engaged with the First and Fourth Brigades, Covington moved forward with his Third Brigade against Morrison's right. After crossing the 20-foot ravine the Americans took fire from Pearson's small force. It was a deadly volley which mortally wounded Covington. Despite the casualties, Colonel Cromwell Pearce commanding the 16th Infantry Regiment, took over and continued the attack pushing back Pearson's detachment.[224]

Having dealt with the American's on his left flank, Morrison now observed the threat on his right flank. He ordered the 49th "in that direction in Echelon followed by the 89th" to meet this new assault. The Americans opened up on them with "a heavy but irregular fire".[225]. The disciplined British firepower began take its toll on the Americans. The Royal Artilley guns added to the American bluecoat's misery. Pearson and Barnes troops soon began to add their firepower against the Americans. The 3rd Brigade now under Pearce, taking heavy casualties and running low on ammunition, fell back across to the east side of ravine.[226]

It was well after 3:00 P.M. when Lieutenant Henry Irvine's two 6-pounders guns arrived on the field aided by the ability of Colonel Swift. Unlimbering along the ravine, Irvine's guns opened up on the 49th and 89th with a destructive fire. Four more guns under the command of Lieutenant Henry Knox Craig were on their way. When they arrived they crossed to the west side of the ravine which was no easy chore and opened up on the 49th with grape and cannister.[227]

"Having again opened his fire upon us, I perceived that it would be impossible, in our advanced position, to stand long against the grape from his field-pieces, which it was accordingly determined to charge," later wrote Harvey. "The 49th was then directed to charge their Guns posted opposite to ours," commented Morrison. Harvey added that the 89th advanced in echelon in support of the 49th.[228] The 49th under the command Lieutenant-Colonel Plenderleath, pushed forward through ploughed ground and had to pull down two snake rail fences to get at the enemy 120 yards away. The American guns began to take its toll on the 49th who lost half their men either killed or wounded. Plenderleath knowing to continue to advance on the guns would be ruinous, ordered his men to full back still under American artillery fire, reform and return fire.[229]

With the guns exposed on the west side of the ravine, while the American troops were on the east side, Craig was ordered to get his guns out of there. To help them the 2nd Regiment of United States Light Dragoons was ordered forward. "I saw a squadron of cavalry galloping up the high road towards our right front," later wrote Lieutenant John Sewell with Plenderleath's troops. The dragoons took fire from the British guns, as well as Barnes and Pearson's men, but continued on. Plenderleath's right company, the target of Woodford's dragoons charge, meanwhile, wheeled back on their left and let loose a deadly volley. Horses and riders went down under the hail of musket balls. Some dragoons returned fire, while others reined their horses back toward the ravine. Despite the 30 killed and wounded, Woodford's charge did buy time for Craig to get his three guns away safely. His fourth gun was captured by the British troops.[230]

Morrison's troops advanced toward the Americans, who began to withdraw for the cover of the trees behind them. As the three brigades were preparing to retreat, reinforcements in the form of the boat guard arrived under the command of Lieutenant-Colonel Timothy Upham arrived. As Boyd rode off with his beaten brigades, Upham with 600 men was left alone to face the advancing British and Canadians. Harvey commented on the conclusion of the battle that "the steady countenance of the troops, finally drove the enemy out of the field; and about half-past four o'clock he gave up the contest and retreated rapidly through the woods, covered by his light troops." Morrison added that the American light infantry "were soon driven away by a judicious movement by L^t. Col^l Pearson."[231]

When Boyd and his men retreated to Cook's tavern, they found that many of the boat crews had already pushed off in their boats. His troops embarked as well and moved four miles down river through cold and stormy weather with snow and sleet and put in on the American side of the river, above the Long Sault Rapids for the night around 9 P.M.. The wounded were taken ashore and put into barns and log houses. The artillery still on the Canadian side of the river, meanwhile, was ordered to be escorted by the dragoons along the King's Highway to Cornwall.[232]

It had been a bloody day for the Americans who suffered around 107 killed and 237 wounded, with roughly 100 captured. Morrison force was also bloodied suffering 22 killed, 148 wounded and 9 missing.[233] Along the banks of the upper St. Lawrence River, one of the biggest battles of the war was over.

CHAPTER 9
DISCONTENT ALONG THE UPPER ST. LAWRENCE
1814

On November 12, the day after the battle, Wilkinson's flotilla shoved off from the New York side of the river and shot the Long Sault Rapids. They rendezvoused at Barnhart's Islands where they were joined by Brown's command, along with the dragoons and artillery traveling overland from Cook's Tavern. It was here that Wilkinson received bad news from Hampton and learned of his defeat at Chateauguay. Hampton also revealed that he would not be joining Wilkinson, stating that his men would only be adding to Wilkinson's supply problems. Instead Hampton promised Wilkinson that he would send supplies by packhorses, the roads not being passable for carts and wagons during the winter. In light of this revelation, Wilkinson held a council of war to discuss the next course of events. Due to the lateness of the season it was decided that an attack on Montreal should be abandoned and the army should go into winter quarters near French Mills, New York. "At this place," wrote Major General Lewis to his wife, "which is situated at the northern boundary of the State and above six miles from the St. Lawrence, terminates our northern campaign for the year."[234] The dragoons crossed the river and rode onto Utica, while the rest of the army in their flotilla headed to French Mills, along the Salmon River arriving there around 3 A.M.. The campaign to take Montreal and strangle off supplies to Upper Canada was over.

After the battle, Crysler's house was converted into a hospital filled with wounded from both sides. Dunlop, a surgeon with the 89th, who arrived after the battle to deal with the human carnage found he had difficulty from keeping the local inhabitants from cramming the patients with food. Many of the locals believed the wounded could only regain their strength from nourishment, to which Dunlop disagreed. He believed a light or weak diet was better. Dunlop was also careful not to leave the American wounded near the Loyalist inhabitants as their "hatred to the Americans was deep-rooted and hearty". This was due to their being persecuted harshly by the Americans during the American Revolution. This might have been an overstatement as one older woman, Mary Whitmore Hoople[235] and her servant girl attempted to nurse back a U.S. rifleman wounded at Hoople Creek. Despite her efforts the soldier died and she made sure he had a decent burial. She would later be given $600 by the American government when they learned of her efforts.[236] Another soldier who did not survive his wounds was a young Canadian officer named Lieutenant Daniel Claus of the 49th. He had been quite sick before the battle, but still took part in the engagement. He was wounded in the ankle by grape shot while advancing against the American guns. On the night of the 11th, he had his lower leg amputated. He was put in a room with nine other men of the 89th and was not well cared for. A month later he required a second amputation and died on December 10.[237]

Besides the wounded, there were a number of prisoners captured, some before and after the battle. Samuel Adams of Fraser's Light Dragoons captured some prisoners on the day of the battle. Having no duty assigned to him, Adams in the early morning had headed behind the American lines. Reaching the King's Highway, he spotted American dragoons galloping along the road. Adams jumped down behind an old log and let them pass within a few feet of him unobserved. Relived that he not been spotted, Adams soon discovered men walking along the road. He stayed behind the log until he identified the men coming as two American officers. Adams stepped out on the road and with his unloaded musket leveled at the officers took them prisoner. Taking their pistols, he took them back to British headquarters and would later be rewarded with two U.S. dragoons horses for his exploit. More prisoners were round up on the evening of the battle at Nudel Bush, located a couple of miles from the battlefield, by Ensign Snyder, George Cook and some other Dundas militia. They captured 14 frightened American soldiers who had plunged deep into the forest attempting to escape the Mohawk warriors.

Commissariat Thomas Ridout, who was on the battlefield on

November 12, said it "was covered with Americans killed and wounded; we had buried some, and about eighty lay dead, some scalped. Some horses were intermingled among them."[238] Some of the American dead found after the battle where bloated with honey oozing from their mouths, noses and reportedly ears. They had apparently gorged themselves on the 100 beehives at a nearby farm. Fifty soldiers were buried in one large grave on a sandy roll near Nine Mile Road. Another 15 were buried in a common grave by the river in an orchard. Thirty more were buried on a local farm, while the rest were mostly buried where they fell.[239]

The British continued to watch the Americans. Writing to Colonel Baynes on November 15 from Milles Roches, Morrison stated that he had received information from Mr. Sheik (possibly Captain David Sheek of the 1st Regiment Stormont Militia) that the Americans had gone 8 miles up the Salmon River. Morrison reported that Mulcaster had gotten his gunboats through the Long Sault Rapids and that his force had been reinforced with the light company of 103rd Foot and a company of Royal Marines. It was also reported that a local inhabitant had his home plundered and although it was impossible to discover the offenders, a sergeant of the Voltigeurs was "in confinement for having some of the articles in his possession."[240]

Harvey writing the following day to Baynes as well, reported that from the information he had gotten from six militiamen "who were taken across by the enemy and who left the enemy at sunset last night" was that "the whole of Wilkinson's army, is at the French Mills" and had "upwards of 1000 workmen were turned out last night with spades and pickaxes for the purpose, they conceive, of throwing up some entrenchments."[241]

French Mills consisted of only six houses, two of which were now being used by the American army as hospitals. A surgeon with the army, Dr. Lovell, described the country around French Mills as wilderness. "Huts and hospitals were necessary to render the army comfortable," he stated. Lovell added that it took several weeks to build these huts. Until they were constructed, the soldiers were living in tents. Another medical man, Surgeon Amasa Trowbridge of 21st Infantry, reported that the weather turned "intensely severe and remained so till the 23d of January." There was a shortage of military supplies, such as tents, blankets, provisions, clothing and medical supplies for the first month. Trowbridge stated that nearest supply of medical stores "could not be obtained short of Albany, a distance of 250 miles.... Under these circumstances, sickness and mortality was very great, and excited general alarm."[242]

Wilkinson soon passed command over to Lewis due his continuing sickness and went to Malone 17 miles away. Lewis, who had also been sick for part of the campaign, took a leave of absence as did Boyd. Command fell to Brown, although Wilkinson was in constant communication with him. As Harvey reported breastworks were constructed in case of attack. Mulcaster writing to Yeo on December 20 from Coteau du Lac wrote that the Americans had three encampments of 1,500 men within a "half a musket shot" of their boats. There was also a blockhouse "with about 50 pieces of cannon around it."[243]

As it "was impossible for the gunboats to proceed up the river," Mulcaster wanting to destroy the American flotilla attempted it "by means of carcasses [a hollow case shell filled with incendiary material] conveyed in a canoe." Midshipman John Harvey and seaman George Barnet volunteered to make the attempt. They paddled up the Salmon River, slipping past the American posts and managed to place a carcass in one of the enemy gunboats and were just about to fire it, when the ice broke around the boat. The two men were quickly discovered by a sentinel who gave the alarm and they had to give up the attempt of destroying the boats for now.

A few days later, information from several American deserters led Mulcaster to believe that "the enemy's magazine, situated in the middle of their encampment, might be blown up." Harvey and Barnett volunteered to make the attempt along with Midshipman George Hawkesworth. Supplied "with combustible matter", the three men crossed over to the New York and hid out in the woods for a few days watching and waiting for an opportunity to strike, but found the magazine heavier guarded then first thought. Not wanting to give up the attempt, Harvey headed into the American camp in disguise. He remained there two days but was betrayed by his conductor to Brown. Fortunately for Midshipman Harvey he escaped as Mulcaster believed he would have been executed otherwise.[244]

By early January conditions had greatly improved at the American camp. Brown managed to get 2,000 new shoes and flannel shirts for the men. Sleighs laden with supplies were bringing their goods in from Utica and Sackets Harbor. By mid-February, Wilkinson received orders from the Secretary of War that the camp at French Mills should be abandoned. Brown was to take 2,000 troops and go to Sackets Harbor. The rest of the troops were to be sent to Plattsburg.[245] The British and Canadians, meanwhile, would soon be paying them a visit to take advantage of their supplies.

"There are two most valuable men with this little army, whose services we are all most anxious to bring under the notice of His Excellency the Commander of the Forces," wrote Lieutenant Colonel Harvey to Baynes on November 16 from Cornwall. The two men were militia captains - William Gilkison and Reuben Sherwood. "They have both been eminently useful by their local knowledge and unswerving exertions ever since the troops left Prescott. . . ." Harvey thought Sherwood was the best man he had met in the country with:

"the best qualified for an appointment, which I would strongly recommend to His Excellency immediately to make (under whatever remuneration he may think proper) for superintending and organizing the procuring of secret intelligence. In India the quartermaster general of the army was at the head of the department (as I think should be the case here) and he had a captain of guides under him, who retained and employed such inferior agents, hercanahs, &c., as he thought proper, and who were paid by and known only to him."

Such an establishment would provided early and "correct information of every movement and plan of the enemy." Harvey continued:

"Captain Sherwood, who in point of and extent of landed property is a man of princely possessions, and who must stand or fall with the country, not only as being marked by the enemy but as being inherently and hereditarily loyal, I would recommend to be employed in this way with some adequate salary, say 10s. or 15s. per diem, with his military pay, and to be accountable for other disbursements to the quartermaster and adjutant general of the army, or such other officer as Sir George might think fit to direct, Captain Sherwood is a good draftsman."[246]

It was not long before Sherwood was active in his new position with the Quartermaster General's Department. Not all the goods were handed over from Hamilton as agreed on November 10 when Morrison and Mulcaster paid the village a visit. Some of the goods were at Madrid on the Grass River and were advertised for sale "for the benefit of the American Government." Sherwood submitted a plan to Morrison to recover the British property which the British officer approved.

On the night of February 6, 1814, Sherwood with "a subaltern officer, two sergeants and twenty rank and file of the Royal Marines, together with ten soldiers of the Incorporated Militia at Prescott under Captain Kerr," crossed over the St. Lawrence River at Iroquois Point. He led his small party to Hamilton at midnight and posted guards to prevent resistance and "impressed all the sleighs and horses he could find". They then pushed 14 miles deeper to where the goods were deposited at Madrid along the Grass River. As there was not enough sleighs to take all the goods, Sherwood left behind some of the effects, mostly of minor value. He would not allow the building these goods were housed in to be torched, fearing private property might be destroyed as well.

With the sleighs loaded by 4:30 A.M., Sherwood headed back to Hamilton. On passing through Hamilton, not a house was entered, nor anybody hurt or their property taken. At 2 P.M. they reached the river, where Lieutenant Shaver of the 1st Dundas Regiment of Militia was waiting for them in boats. The local American militia meanwhile had rallied to pursue the raiders but had come on some "very agreeable mixed liquor" called "shrub" left by Sherwood where they would be sure to find it. This ended the pursuit except for some of the enemy militia who were handily dispersed by the Royal Marines. The whole party crossed to the Canadian side of the river with no casualties.[247]

More raids were to follow along the Salmon River when it was known, thanks to Sherwood of the American plans to evacuate French Mills. On February 14, Morrison and Lieutenant Colonel Scott of the 103rd Foot led a raid down to French Mills and captured a large amount of property left by the Americans. Not having the means to bring off the goods, Major Cockburn of the Canadian

Fencibles was provided with sleighs and ordered to get the plunder. Five days later another raiding party left for the Salmon River and Malone. This force consisted of around 500 men under Scott and over a 100 sleighs, many from Dundas County. Scott's raiders torched the enemy boats and barracks at French Mills, then part of them pushed on for Malone, while the rest of the raiders headed for Four Corners.

A large amount of stores and ammunition were taken from these places, as were all the pork, beef, flour and whiskey the troops could carry. What could not be taken was destroyed. On the journey home, the officers had a hard time keeping discipline among some of the raiders as there was a great deal of revelry among them. One teamster was carrying a hogshead of whiskey in his sleigh, which the troops behind him had bored a hole in with a bayonet. The soldiers would then run up and fill a gallon jug and return to their comrades and enjoy its content. On crossing the river, the ice broke beneath one of the heavy laden sleighs, causing it and its horses to be swept under the ice. Fortunately the passengers managed to jump off in time. Once back in Upper Canada, the teamsters were ordered to leave their sleighs in view of a local hotel under heavy guard. This was done as a precaution so the teamsters, who had been enjoying the whiskey, would not take their plunder home instead of to the government depot at Cornwall.[248]

Another raid under Scott again was launched on February 24, but this time the raiders didn't get much plunder. In May, the prize money for the raids was distributed by the Military Secretary and Prize Agent Noah Freer. For the raid on February 14 and 15, the soldiers share amounted to 13 shillings per private, while the latter two raids rewarded a private with 5 shillings and 6 pence.[249]

Much of the provisions that came into British hands from the United States did not come through raids. Most was delivered across the border by the Americans themselves in a lucrative illicit cross border trade. Prevost writing to Bathhurst in August, 1814 stated that "two-thirds of the army in Canada are at this moment eating beef provided by American contractors, drawn principally from the States of Vermont and New York." The cattle moving north across the border into Lower Canada was described by one person as looking like "herds of buffalo." As early as December 1812, the American commander at Salmon River was allowing flour to be taken to

Cornwall.[250]

In Upper Canada there were thousands of soldiers, sailors and Indians to be fed. Kingston by the fall of 1813 had 5,000 men to feed. Thomas Ridout, who was to be posted at Cornwall in January 1814, wrote to his father:

"To-morrow I return to Cornwall to take charge of my new post. There are 1,600 troops there to be fed, and my duty will be hard, for the country is so excessively poor that our supplies are all drawn from the American side of the river. They drive droves of cattle from the interior under pretence of supplying the army at Salmon river, and are so allowed to pass the guards, and at night cross them over to our side. I shall also be under the necessity of getting most of my flour from their side."[251]

Surgeon Dunlap who was posted at Cornwall in the spring of 1814, recounted how an American cattle drover from Vermont arrived at Cornwall to sell his livestock. Meeting with a colonel, the Vermont drover hearing the officer wanted cattle stated that he "just brought a hundred on 'em across at St. Regis, as fine critters, Colonel, as ever had hair on 'em." Satisfied with the price offered by the Commissary, the Vermonter said that a friend of his had 300 more who belonged "to his father, who is our Senator."[252]

Ridout also wrote on June 19, 1814 from Cornwall on the high position of authority of some of the American drovers: "I have contracted with a Yankee magistrate to furnish this post with fresh beef. A major came with him to make the agreement, but, as he was foreman to the grand jury at the court in which the government prosecutes the magistrates for high treason and smuggling, he turned his back and would not see the paper signed."[253]

Further upriver at Ogdensburg there was a very brisk trade going on, much of this due to David Parish. Parish's agents had a good relations with the British officers at Prescott. Parish's nephew, John Ross, was a guest of Macdonell for dinner, while Judge Ford of Ogdensburg had British officers for dinner guests on his side of the river. Morrison supplied Ross with a handbill on news from Europe. Of importance to the British was the livestock crossing the border. Ross writing to his uncle on July 23, 1813: "It is incredible what quantities of cattle & sheep are driven into Canada. We can hardly get any for love or money, the day before yesterday upwards of 100 Oxen went through Prescott, yesterday about 200."[254]

After the battle at Ogdensburg in February 1813, relations returned to normal, with Upper Canadians crossing the river to frequent the Parish's store. Ross, wrote less than a month after Macdonell's attack, "The people from the other side are constantly crossing. They come in quest of tea principally . . . ."[255] Ogdensburg, was at the mercy of the British in which the redcoats promised not to bother them as long they behaved themselves.

The American army was greatly concerned over this cross border traffic. Forsyth, according to Ridout writing from Cornwall, had in early 1814 destroyed "all the boats up the river, to prevent supplies coming over."[256] This did little to stop the smuggling.

Major-General George Izard, who replaced Wilkinson in March 1814 and commanded the reorganized Right Division of the 9th Military Division (Brown commanded the Left Division), wrote to the Secretary of War informing him of the situation: "From the St. Lawrence to the ocean an open disregard prevails for the laws prohibiting intercourse with the enemy. The roads to St. Regis is covered with droves of cattle and the river with rafts destined for the enemy. The revenue officers see these things but acknowledge their inability to put a stop to such outrageous proceedings."[257]

Izard offered to supply the Collectors at Plattsburg and Burlington, Vermont with men and means, but found when the "time of exertion arrives the civil officers decline acting." Izard recommended: "Nothing but a cordon of troops from the French Mills to Lake Memphramagog could effectually check the evil." Without these supplies Izard continued: "the British forces in Canada would soon be suffering from famine, or their government be subjected to immense expense for their maintenance."[258] He was right and the British knew it.

The procuring of food to keep their troops fed, despite the livestock coming across the border, forced the British to take action along the Upper St. Lawrence. John Green, the Deputy Assistant Commissary General at Prescott, in March of 1813 concerned over a grain shortage, advised that the militia should be allowed to return home to put in a spring crop. He also added that no grain should be exported to Lower Canada. Green's successor, Thomas Osborne, went further by sending detachments of militiamen to help in the thrashing of wheat. In April of 1814, Osborne was recommending that the farms of those who had deserted to the enemy should be seized and cultivated. The deserter's livestock should be taken as well.[259]

A much more drastic measure was taken in November 1813, when De Rottenburg introduced martial law in the Midland, Johnstown and Eastern districts to keep farmers from withholding their produce for a better price. Not surprisingly the local farmers did not take kindly to this measure, even though De Rottenburg thought he was offering fair prices for their provisions. Upper Canadians were firm believers in property rights and it angered them that now the British authorities could simply seize what they wanted. What made matters worse, was that despite the promise of pay, many farmers did not get any money for their goods or not the full value. Some of the problem lay in the seizing of food without permission by the commissariat department.[260]

De Rottenburg was replaced in December 1813 by Lieutenant General Gordon Drummond. He was born in Quebec in 1772 where his father was deputy paymaster general to the British forces. In 1789, Drummond became a ensign in the 1st Foot and in the coming years would see action in the Netherlands and Egypt. He went onto serve in Gibraltar and Jamaica, before coming to the Canadas in 1807. In late 1812 he was transferred to Ireland, but returned to Lower Canada in early November 1813, but was ordered to take command in Upper Canada which he did on December 13. In Upper Canada, Drummond revoked the extremely unpopular martial law, believing the onslaught of winter and bad roads had prevented the farmers from selling their goods to the British.[261] He was wrong.

In March, the House of Assembly voted on censuring De Rottenburg for resorting to martial law which they believed to be unconstitutional with intentions of destroying the laws of Upper Canada.[262] Drummond was not long in having to invoke martial law again not only for the eastern part of the province but for all of it. The food situation at Kingston, for example, was becoming critical as the garrison consumed almost 5,000 rations daily. At one point there was only 16 barrels of flour left in store. The head of the commissariat urged Drummond to take this drastic step or "otherwise the necessary supplies could not on terms be obtained." Drummond ordered that the officers and agents gathering the supplies "should observe the greatest moderation and use their best endeavours to conciliate the people . . ." and offer a fair price for goods taken. Nevertheless, Drummond knew that the Assembly would try to censure him as they did De Rottenburg and asked sanction and support from his superiors.[263]

Martial law or no martial law, farmers along the Upper St. Lawrence at times had their produce taken by British soldiers and sailors. In Cornwall, which saw a lot of military traffic and personnel, it was advisable for the local inhabitants to give the produce of their gardens or orchards away freely or else the soldiers would help themselves. A party of seamen one night killed a calf and ate it only to discover the next morning from the hoofs that had actually consumed a colt[264].

Drummond was also concerned over the cross border traffic existing in places like Prescott and Ogdensburg and the military information that might be passing to the Americans. To curtail this movement, he attempted to put severe restrictions on it in late 1813. After complaints by Gilkison, who was attempting to get pork and flour from Ogdensburg, Prevost intervened. To control the cross border interaction and yet still keep the much need provisions coming from the Americans, a licensing system was set up for the Upper St. Lawrence region.[265]

All of this did nothing to improve relations between the civilian population and the British military, which had been slowly deteriorating as the war progressed. Some settlers along the Upper St. Lawrence River determined to defend their property, began to see the British more of a threat to their possessions than the Americans. The British officers on the other hand stationed along the Upper St. Lawrence (and other places in the province for that matter) took a dim view of the civilians self-interested behaviour. They interpreted it as a kin to treasonous at times.

Pearson who was stationed at Prescott for a good part of the war had his share of trouble with the local civilians. Some of this trouble was over his impressment order of farmers wagons and horses in mid-1813. Foraging parties were sent out to impress teams and provisions. Some farmers were not happy about this as they had not been paid for earlier impressment of their possessions, as well some farmers not close by simply sent their horses to be used by the militia stationed at Prescott. The militiamen in charge of these horses at times were less then attentive of the animals and let them wander off. Other times even when the farmers were with their horses, they were not happy about the British officers overworking them and their animals. Daniel Jones, justice of the peace at Brockville, by 1814 was beginning to refuse to sign warrants allowing British officers to impress local horses, under the excuse they did not have adequate credentials for what they wanted them for. He also feared law suits from the farmers for any losses they might suffer.

There were wrangles over the licensing to trade as well as abuses of the system. Two men with a license to trade were captured moving a deserter's property across the St. Lawrence River. Hiram Spafford, the merchant who successfully sued Fraser during Wilkinson's campaign, had his license to trade across the river revoked by Pearson as did Daniel Jones. Both men were from Brockville. Pearson might have been suspicious of these men because although they had licenses, no provisions ever ended up at the Commissariat. In the case of Spafford, Pearson wanted him removed from the militia claiming that he was an American who only been in the province two years and had only taken the oath of allegiance for one year. Jones, dissatisfied with losing his license, complained to Drummond informing the British commander that at times he collected information on the Americans for the commander at Prescott, as well procuring provisions for the military. Jones believed Pearson actions had been influenced by "private friends". Amongst others, this might have included Gilkison who of course was involved in the cross border trade at Prescott. Gilkison, along with Colonels Thomas Fraser, Joel Stone and Dr. Solomon Jones had earlier complained to Drummond's civil secretary of the intelligence being passed to the Americans from between Brockville and Morristown. They recommended that trade be stopped between the two towns. Drummond was already not pleased with the area between Brockville and Gananoque which he stated was "infested by swarms of disaffected people" who were in communication with the Americans.[266]

Another problem the British found with the Upper Canadian population was the reluctance of a fair number to serve in the militia. Desertion was high among the various militia regiments in Upper Canada. Many did not desert to the enemy, just simply went home to tend to their farms. Others found they could make much more money working as civilian laborers for the King rather than serving in the militia. Along the Upper St. Lawrence, the 2nd Leeds Regiment of Militia under Colonel Joel Stone for example had a desertion rate of about 25%. At times it spiked much higher than that. During the course of the war, about 103 men from this regiment deserted to the Americans. Roughly one in four men. Refusing to march with the militia or leaving without permission could incur a fine or a stint in gaol, but deserting to the enemy was a much more dangerous undertaking that could lead to the death penalty.[267]

Two man captured for deserting to the enemy were tried in a general court martial at Kingston that ran from December 6th to the 11th. Private Amos McIntyre on the Incorporated Militia was charged with deserting to the enemy from Prescott on July 4, 1813. He was captured at Ogdensburg a little over two months later. He was found guilty and was sentenced to be shot on December 20 in front of the garrison at Kingston. The second man was private Joseph Seely also of the Incorporated Militia. He was charged with deserting on August 28, 1813 from Prescott to the enemy and was brought back a prisoner on November 20, 1813. He had a second charge against him for "assisting in piloting one of the enemy's boats down the river St. Lawrence . . .." Apparently he had been one of the many Canadian pilots used by Wilkinson. For the first charge of desertion he was found guilty and was "to be transported for the term and space of seven years as a felon, to such a place as His Honor the President or person administering the Government of the Province of Upper Canada shall be pleased direct." He was acquitted on the second charge for lack of evidence.[268]

Bringing back a deserter from "his Majesty's Regular Forces" could be worth the effort as the British were paying £5 per deserter.[269] Sometimes deserters were brought in dead. In early March 1813, two soldiers from the Glengarry Light Infantry deserted from Kingston headed for Sackets Harbor across the ice. They never made it as four Indians and two militiamen tracked them down and killed them when they attempted to resist.[270]

CHAPTER 10
OSWEGO AND THE END OF THE WAR
1814

Shipbuilding continued at Kingston as the war for Lake Ontario was in part one of a shipbuilders. Despite virtually having no navy on the lake at the start of the war, the Americans at Sackets were winning the war of building ships now having more sailors and guns then the Royal Navy at Kingston. Yeo met to do something about that.

Improvements were made on the naval facilities at Kingston and work began in the fall of 1813 on building two frigates. Despite a near strike, work progressed well on the ships that a third frigate was started when it was rumored the Americans were building more ships at Sackets. This third ship would become the massive *St. Lawrence*. More gunboats were also constructed.

To man the ships, Yeo received the welcome reinforcements of 180 Royal Navy officers and seamen in mid-December 1813. In late March, 1814, over 200 more Royal Navy personnel arrived from an overland march from New Brunswick. Two companies of Royal Marines were transferred from Prescott to Kingston to serve on Yeo's squadron. To replace the marines, two companies from the 89th Foot were ordered to Prescott from Cornwall.[271]

While ships were being built to gain control of Lake Ontario, American commissioners left for Europe in January to began peace talks with the British at the proposal of Russia. The war in Europe was going badly for Napoleon as his gamble against Russia failed; the British, Spanish and Portugese forces had pushed his troops out of the Iberian Peninsula; and he suffered a serious defeat at the battle of Leipzig. Soon the British would be able to send a large number of troops to North America.

In North America, talk of exchanging prisoners began while an armistice proposed by the American government was turned down by Prevost as he did not have the authority to accept it. Prevost was told by the British government in London to continue the war as Great Britain met to make a peace with the Americans that would be to their advantage.

At Kingston, Drummond was skeptical of the armistice proposed by the Americans believing only they would reap the advantages of it by giving them time to built up their forces. Secondly, if the Americans wanted a "cessation of hostilities" reasoned Drummond, it was because the advantage of the coming campaign lay with the British. Yeo agreed with this reasoning believing that it was "by no means certain the Enemy will have the advantage at the commencement of the Campaign" on Lake Ontario. With the reinforcement of seamen, two new frigates and with the third frigate being built which Yeo believed was of a "far greater force than any the Enemy can launch at Sacketts Harbour", the Royal Navy Commodore felt confident that he could "bring Chauncey to a decisive action". If Chauncey was too strong, Yeo figured to "manonvre with Him until the third Ship is ready - And which Vessel I look upon to be of a description to look down all opposition."[272]

Drummond believed that with even a temporary naval superiority, Sackets Harbor should be attacked in a combined arms operation with the purpose of destroying the American fleet there. To pull off such an operation 4,000 troops would be needed. Besides attacking Sackets, Drummond thought an attack against the American naval depot at Oswego should be made. If the stores there could be destroyed, it would slow down Chauncey's ship building endeavors at Sackets Harbor. Prevost was against the idea of attacking Sackets, reasoning that if Drummond needed 4,000 troops for the attack, the present force at Kingston would have to be strengthened "to at least five thousand effective." This would only add to "the great difficulties" Drummond was having in obtaining provisions and forage to maintain his current number of troops. Secondly, Prevost did not want to send that many regulars from Lower Canada leaving the province's defences to provincials and militia. Also Prevost wrote that the "views of His Majesty's Government respecting the mode of conducting the war with America, do not justify my exposing too much on one shake. It is by war measures and occasional daring enterprizes with apparently disproportionate means, that the character of the war has been sustained, and from the policy I am not disposed to depart."[273]

On May 3, Drummond wrote to tell Prevost of his setting out for a raid against Oswego to destroy the naval stores there "as soon as the wind is fair." Information received from Sackets Harbor on April 28 brought news that the American's were building a new ship to be finished in six weeks. "If such be the case," wrote Drummond, "it is impossible for us to keep pace with such exertions." Drummond again repeated that Sackets must be attacked to be able to "completely secure the Upper Province." For the present attack against Oswego, Drummond's force consisted of 450 men from De Watteville Regiment, 50 Glengarry Light Infantry, 350 Marines, 20 sappers, a detachment of Royal Artillery numbering 24 men and 6 Rocketeers. In all 900 men.[274]

At 5 A.M. the following day, Yeo's squadron of seven ships and a handful of gunboats carrying the troops sailed out of the harbour at Kingston. It was 5 P.M. before they were out of sight from Kingston. With the winds being variable they did not arrive off Oswego until noon of May 5.[275]

Oswego was guarded by an old British fort built in the mid-18th century, now partly in ruins and surrounded by a ditch, located on a hill on the east side of the Oswego River. On the opposite bank lay the town. On April 30, Lieutenant-Colonel George Mitchell with a little less than 300 men from the 3rd U.S. Artillery had arrived to establish the defences there. In the old fort he had five old cannons, over half of which had no trunnions. There were also a few militia companies as well as 25 U.S. Navy personnel under Commandant Melanchton Woolsey. This naval contingent had come to move the naval stores which were stored 13 miles upriver at Oswego Falls. The supplies had been brought there after a long journey up the Hudson and Mohawk Rivers from New York City, and onto the Oswego River. From the Oswego River they were to be loaded onto schooners and bateaux for the journey to Sackets.[276]

When the British fleet was spotted, alarms guns were sounded to gather the militia. The British squadron lay "within long Gun shot" of the fort. Mitchell ordered tents taken from the storehouse and pitched in front of the town. He hoped the tents would deceive the British into thinking he had more troops then he did.

The gunboats under Captain Edward Collier RN were sent

into draw American fire so as to determine the number and position of their guns. After the American defenses were reconnoitered, "arrangements were made for its attack" which was to commence at 8 P.M.. Apparently the tents fooled no one. A heavy squall blowing from the northwest canceled the attack as the squadron was forced to stand off about 10 miles from Oswego until the next morning.[277]

When the squadron returned on May 6, the vessels *Montreal* (formerly *Wolfe*) and *Niagara* (formerly *Royal George*) moved in and opened up on the old fort. The old guns there returned fire. The *Princess Charlotte* was longer getting into position and it would be around 1 P.M. before her guns fired on the fort. Meanwhile the *Magent* (formerly *Sidney Smith*) scoured the town and kept watch on the militia who might try to reinforce the fort. The *Charwell* (formerly *Earl of Moira*) and the *Star* (formerly *Lord Melville*) around noon towed in the boats containing the troops.[278] The attack began an hour later. The boats and gunboats moving toward shore were under the command of Captain Richard O'Conner RN. The assault troops, consisting of the Glengarry Light Infantry, the flank companies of the De Watteville Regiment and the 2nd Battalion of the Royal Marines were under the command of Lieutenant Colonel Victor Fischer of the De Watteville Regiment. The rest of the troops were held as reserves on the *Magnet* and *Princess Charlotte*.

Covered by a "stream of grape and canister shot", Fischer's troops were forced to wade in waist deep water to dry land when their boats grounded on shallows quite a piece from shore. Once on shore the troops took fire from American troops positioned in a nearby woods, southeast of the fort, to oppose their landing. More American troops were "drawn up on the Brow of the Hill."[279]

The Glengarry Light Infantry were quickly dispatched to clear the woods, which they did, driving the Americans back to the fort. With this done, the De Wattevilles formed up in line with the Royal Marines on their right. The Glengarry Light Infantry were on the left flank as the red and green coated soldiers advance on the American troops on the slope east of the fort. Witnessing the assault up the eastern slope toward the fort was Yeo and Drummond who had also come ashore.[280]

Moving up the hill, the redcoats took a heavy fire from the Americans, while having a hard time returning fire due to their cartridges getting wet when wading ashore. On the steeper western slop a detachment of 200 seamen under Captain Mulcaster had landed and were pushing up the hill as well. Mulcaster did not get far when he took a wicked wound to his leg, putting him out of action. The seamen charged on.

The assault continued up the east side, breaching over the embankments into the fort. Once inside the fort, Lieutenant John Hewett RN, climbed up the flag and pull down the American flag which had been nailed there. After a determined defence, Mitchell quickly ordered a retreat. The Americans retired in good order, heading through the woods for Oswego Falls. Across the river, Woolsey seeing all was lost, scuttled his remaining schooners and retreated as well. (Another schooner the *Growler* had earlier been scuttled at the mouth of the river.)[281]

It had been a bloody little fight for the British and Canadians troops with 15 killed and 62 wounded. The Royal Navy had also lost 3 killed and 11 wounded. The Americans on the other hand had 6 killed, 38 wounded and 25 missing.[282]

Now in possession of Oswego, Drummond and Yeo's men proceeded to refloat three schooners and the stores they carried. Nine pieces of ordnances were captured, while two were destroyed. Also taken were 70 coils of rope and cordage. Well over a 1,000 barrels of flour, pork, potatoes, salt and tallow were captured. Munitions and stores that could not be carried off where destroyed. The barracks were torched as well and the fort dismantled. By May 8, the troops were back at Kingston. The victory at Oswego was hollow for the British. They had only destroyed or captured a small number of enemy naval stores which did little to slow the ship building at Sackets Harbor. Had they pushed up the Oswego River they could have captured a lot more guns.[283]

Morrison, commanding at Fort Wellington, which the fort a Prescott had been named in early 1814, sent information to Drummond at Kingston he received on Sackets not long afterwards. A few days before the attack on Oswego, 70 guns had arrived there for the new ship being built at Sackets Harbor. The guns and stores had been sent upriver for safety during the attack. The informant had no doubt that the Americans would make every effort to get the guns to Sackets. He also reported that a new brig was ready, while another one would be in 12 days and another ship, currently in stocks, would be launched in 20 days. A larger ship being constructed would not be ready for a month.[284]

    Yeo was soon back to set up a blockade of Sackets Harbor. Despite the presence of the Royal Navy ships, Woolsey attempted to bring 19 boats loaded with guns and cables for the new ships at Sackets. His plan was to reach Sandy Creek, located about 12 miles south of Sackets, and move the supplies overland to the naval base. At sunset on May 28, Woolsey reached Oswego, having moved up river from Oswego Falls. Acting as escort were 120 riflemen under Major David Appling. Rowing all night most of the boats reached Salmon Creek on the morning of the 29th. Alarmingly, one boat was missing.[285]

    Reinforced by 120 Oneida Indians who moved along the shore, Woolsey did not linger long at Salmon River. Fearing the missing boat would reveal to the British his intentions and location, Woolsey pushed on and reached Sandy Creek at noon. The missing large boat, carrying two 24-pounders and a 19 and half inch cable, was pushing onto Sackets instead of heading for Sandy Creek. The boat was soon picked up by the Royal Navy and as feared by Woolsey, the British soon learned of his plan.[286]

    Captain Stephen Popham RN with two gunboats and three cutters set out to intercept Woolsey's convoy. Captain Francis Spilsbury RN was later sent out as well. The combined force, which numbered about 200 sailors and marines, discovered the American boats at Sandy Creek on the morning of the 30th. Small parties were landed on either side of the creek as the gunboats pushed up the waterway. The gunboats fired grape and cannister into the bushes in hopes of preventing an ambush. It didn't work.

    Woolsey and Appling set up their sailors, riflemen and Indians in an ambush about half a mile from where their boats were landed. Reinforcement consisting of a squadron of dragoons and light artillery from Sackets were stationed near the boats. The Americans sprung the ambush which completely bagged Popham's force. The British suffered 18 killed and 50 wounded, with the rest captured. The Americans had only 2 men wounded. The stores reached Sackets Harbor safely.[287]

    It was not longer afterwards that the Royal Navy's blockade of Sackets was lifted on June 5. The summer of 1814 would see no decisive naval actions on Lake Ontario. Chauncey would do a poor job in supporting Brown's invasion of the Niagara Peninsula. The ship builders at Kingston, meanwhile, laboured to complete the massive three decker 102 gun *St. Lawrence*.

Building this ship would stretch British supply line on the St. Lawrence River as material and guns would have to be taken upriver for its construction. On May 1, Ridout writing from Cornwall stated that: "Every day twelve batteaux arrive here from Lachine on their way to Kingston, with provisions and naval stores, and we have troops stationed along the river to protect the communication." Besides the *St. Lawrence*, parts for a prefabricated ship were also sent upriver to be later assembled at Kingston.[288]

Protecting the communication lines was put to the test in mid June, when Sailing Master Francis Gregory with 20 men headed out of Sackets Harbor in three gigs with intentions of attacking the enemy's supply bateaux bound for Kingston. Letting troop laden convoys pass by, Gregory with his small contingent of men moved on the British gunboat *Blacksnake* under militia Captain Landon carrying 20 Royal Marines near Tar Island, located not far from modern Rockport, Ontario.

Landon spotted one of the American vessels and mistakenly thought it was British. Climbing into a small skiff, he went to meet the American vessel and boarded it. He was quickly taken prisoner. His gunboat crew seeing Landon go aboard, assumed the vessel was friendly and pulled toward her when the rest of the American vessels made their appearance and captured the *Blacksnake*. The Americans quickly headed for French Creek with their prize.

Before Gregory reached French Creek, he soon found himself being pursued by another gunboat armed with a carronade and 18 men under Lieutenant Campbell of 104th Foot. A few shots were fired against the Americans from Campbell's gunboat forcing Gregory to abandon the *Blacksnake*. Rowing as hard as they could, Gregory's vessels managed to outdistance the British gunboat and escaped around Gravelly Point. The *Blacksnake*, now back in British hands with most of her stores, was taken to Kingston.[289]

Another small action in the summer of 1814 (probably sometime in August), saw Captain Thomas Fraser with 60 men cross the St. Lawrence River from Upper Canada landing somewhere above Morrisville, near Hammond. Fraser headed onto Rossie located 10 miles south of the St. Lawrence River to capture horse thieves said to be in the area. At the time of Fraser's visit, a justice's court was being held which was quickly dissolved. The horse thieves sought were not found, but Fraser did make inquires about an iron furnace being built. After getting a pledge from the proprietors that no munitions would be cast there, Fraser and his men headed home. A plan to attack Fraser was discussed by the residents, but it was dropped for fear of reprisal.[290]

This was the last action of any consequence on the Upper St. Lawrence. On September 10, the 194 foot *St. Lawrence* was launched, but would not be ready for action until early October. When she finally sailed out of Kingston, control of Lake Ontario reverted to the British as Chauncey took his fleet to Sackets Harbor for safety. The Americans began work on two big ships and had plans for an even bigger third one when word arrived that war had ended in the new year.

The difficulty in moving supplies up the St. Lawrence River during the war caused recommendations to be made for its improvement. Commissary-General Robinson writing to Prevost on November 14, 1814 suggested:

"To render the transportation to Upper Canada a less difficult and thereby save a great part of the labor at present engaged in it, it is to be wished that Measures may be taken for loaded Bateaus to go from Montreal to Fort Wellington and there deliver their loading into Boats, or vessels, of a Larger Size, navigated by proportionably fewer hands, to be taken to Kingston."

He went to recommend a canal be constructed between Montreal and Lachine "under a Scientific Director, acquainted with Canal Making in England . . .." He thought the work could "be accomplished in a short time" and the expense of constructing it would be compensated "by the saving of the Cartage" and by a toll charged to merchants for passage of their bateaux.

At Prescott, Fort Wellington was officially completed in early December. Work on the fort had slowed when De Gaugreben had been sent to York in September 1813. By early May of the following year, the engineer was back at Prescott from the Niagara region. By the end of the month, De Gaugreben had 20 carpenters, 3 masons, 3 blacksmiths, 2 sawyers and 36 privates working away at the fortification. In July, 30 teamsters were earning 4 dollars a day removing earth at the river's edge to built a battery. The battery was completed in late August. Work was not going as fast as De Gaugreben would have liked as he was having problems finding soldiers to work. Fort Wellington during the war saw lots of units stationed there, but many moved on after only a week or two limiting De Gaugreben's work force. By September, however, he was to get steady help when the officers at Fort Wellington had received orders to assist De Gaugreben. The fort upon its completion consisted of a surrounding dry ditch, a rectangular earthworks with the north wall being V shaped. Each corner of the walls mounted heavy guns and there were casements in the ramparts. Behind the earthern ramparts was the single storey blockhouse. Surrounding the fort were pickets. Not all were impressed with the new completed works, as one royal engineer referred to it as "a great mass of earth badly put together."[291]

The war elsewhere had seen thousands of Wellington's veterans come to Lower Canada but squandered in an invasion along Lake Champlain headed by Prevost, when the British fleet on Lake Champlain was severely defeated by the American fleet. Prevost retreated back to Lower Canada. On the other hand the American invasion of the Niagara Peninsula ended in failure when the last troops retreated back to New York in November. On Lake Huron, the British and Indians managed to keep control of the vital fur trade route after a failed American attempt to recapture Michilmackinac. The British also had success on the eastern seaboard where they captured parts of Maine. At Washington, the British burned the public buildings there. In January 1815, the British received a severe defeat at New Orleans. On February 11, 1815, Fort Bowyer guarding the entrance to Mobile, Alabama surrendered to the British. This was one of the last actions of the war, which unbeknownst to the combatants a peace treaty ending the war had been signed on December 24, 1814. The treaty however was not binding until both sides ratified it which the British parliament did shortly after Christmas and the American congress did in mid-February. The war officially ended February 17, 1815.[292]

The Treaty of Ghent saw all conquered land handed back to their rightful owners, while peace was to be made with the Indians restoring to them their possessions and rights they had prior to the war. Three commissions were to later determine the international boundary between the United States and British North America. Also it was agreed that both Great Britain and the United States would do their best to end the slave trade. No mention was made to the maritime issues which started the war.[293]

CHAPTER 11
THE RETURN OF PEACE
1815 AND BEYOND

The inhabitants along the Upper St. Lawrence on either side of the river were fortunate that the bulk of the serious fighting during the war had been in the Niagara Peninsula and the western part of the province, as well into old Northwest of the United States. With the exception of Wilkinson's campaign in November 1813, settlers in the eastern part of Upper Canada were spared massive amounts of destruction of private property as seen elsewhere. Although spared the bulk of the fighting, the Upper St. Lawrence River was arguably the most vital part of the province. Despite the problems that sometimes existed between the British and the Upper Canadians in the area, they had managed to keep Upper Canada's lifeline open which led to the successful defence of the bulk of the province.

What of the post war careers of the men, Canadian, British and American, who played an important role on the Upper St. Lawrence?

John Crysler, whose farm the epic battle was fought on, received property damage to the amount of £400 in compensation in 1816. Throughout the war and afterwards, Crysler continued to serve in the House of Assembly with 1824 being the last time he was elected to the Assembly for Dundas county. In 1818 he had been appointed the collector of customs at Cornwall. In the 1820s and 30s Crysler had financial trouble. Heavily involved in the timber trade, Crysler's men were arrested in 1826 for cutting timber on clergy reserves. In a fifteen year period starting from 1820, Crysler had 28 judgement registered against him, amounting to £12,000. In 1838, Crysler commanded the 1st Regiment of Dundas Militia at the battle of the Windmill. Crysler moved to the northern part of Stormont County and set up a sawmill and gristmill along the South Nation

River in 1843. The town there, Crysler, would be named after him. He died in 1852.[294]

Reuben Sherwood, who had proved so useful and resourceful in the war, returned to surveying at the end of the hostilities. He died in 1851. Unfortunately this remarkable man has had little written about him.

Richard Duncan Fraser was appointed assistant quartermaster general in February 1815, but word of the war's end prevented him from fulfilling his new position. With the coming of peace Fraser took up farming and in 1816 was appointed justice of the peace for the Johnstown District.

In 1817, Fraser received £89 from the government for money he had spent on getting horses shod during the war. The bulk of the money was to cover the lawsuit against Fraser by Hiram Spafford.[295] Fraser soon found himself in court again this time in 1818 for assaulting Robert Gourlay, the Scotsman who was causing political upheaval in Upper Canada at the time, and was fined 40 shillings.

Fraser went on to be elected to the House of Assembly in 1831 for Greenville, where his fiery temper flared again when he threatened to horsewhip William Lyon Mackenzie. The following year, Fraser was appointed customs collector for Brockville. He would go onto become colonel of the 2nd Regiment of Greenville Militia which he led into action at the battle of the Windmill in 1838. Fraser had financial problems in the 1840s and was eventually relived of his position as custom collector. He died in 1857.[296]

William Johnston, the Upper Canadian who had gone over to the Americans in 1813, worked as a smuggler through the 1820s and 30s. During the rebellion in 1837, Johnston offered his services to the Patriots. Participating in a few raids throughout the uprising, Johnston most famous exploit was the capture of the steamship *Sir Robert Peel*, (in which Richard Duncan Fraser was aboard at the time). He intended to use the steamship as a pirate vessel, but lacking enough men to crew it, he burn it instead. Now he had a reward on his head - a £1,000 from Lord Durham and $500 from the New York governor. As "Commander-in-Chief of the naval forces and flotilla" in 1838, Johnston continued to make raids against Canada hoping to start another war between the two countries, with hopes of the American being victorious. Johnston went onto play a naval role in the Hunters invasion of Upper Canada near Prescott which resulted in the battle of the Windmill. Johnston's ship ran aground and he missed out on the battle, which resulted in the defeat and capture of the invaders. Johnston surrendered to the Americans and was put in jail, but was released on bail. He continued with his small raids in the Thousand Islands region. He was captured and jailed again in Albany, but escaped before finishing his one year sentence. Eventually Johnston received a pardon from the American authorities and settled to run a tavern at Clayton and a lighthouse keeper at Rock Island. He died in 1870.[297]

Colonel John Harvey, who played such an important role in the victory at Crysler's Farm, went on to serve with distinction in the fighting in the Niagara Peninsula in 1814. He would eventually be knighted for his war service. In 1824, Harvey returned to England, but his ties with British North America were far from over. He returned to Upper Canada the following year as part of a five man commission who were to determine the price that crown land should be sold to the Canada Company. In 1828, Harvey was in turbulent Ireland as inspector general of police in the province of Leinster. Eight years later he was in Prince Edward Island as the lieutenant governor. In the next 16 years he would serve as lieutenant governor in all the maritime colonies. He died in 1852.

Lieutenant Colonel Joseph Morrison, who commanded the force that dogged Wilkinson, was posted along the St. Lawrence River at Cornwall, Coteau-du-Lac and Prescott following the battle. In 1814, he served in the Niagara Peninsula where he was seriously wounded at the battle of Lundy's Lane. In 1816, he returned to England where he went on half-pay, his wounds not healed enough for active duty with the 1st battalion of the 89th that was sent to India. By 1822, Morrison, now recovered, left for India as a lieutenant colonel in the 44th Foot. Promoted to brigadier general, Morrison went on to take part in the invasion of Burma. It was there Morrison took sick with malaria and decided to return to England, hoping the ocean voyage would help recover his health. He was wrong and died on February 15, 1826 on the journey.[298]

Lieutenant Colonel George Macdonell after his role at Chateauguay, became the commander of all regular and militia troops along the Upper St. Lawrence from Montreal to Kingston in June 1814. Later that year he surveyed the Rideau River and was a supporter of the canal later constructed there. In late 1816 he returned to England and four years later married a wealthy woman that looked after him financially. He spent much of the following years trying to get recognition from the War Office for his role in War of 1812. He died in 1870.[299]

Lieutenant Colonel Thomas Pearson in 1814 went onto serve with distinction in the Niagara Peninsula where he was wounded in September. Pearson remained in the army after the war becoming a lieutenant general in 1841. For his service to king he was knighted. He died in 1847.

Major General James Wilkinson made one more attempt against Lower Canada in March 1814. The action at La Colle Mills was a failure. Relieved of command, Wilkinson returned to Washington to face a court of inquiry for his failed Montreal campaign in which he was acquitted. Wilkinson went on to write an autobiography of his life. In 1821 he headed to Mexico in an attempt to get a grant for land in their northern province of Texas. He died four years later in Mexico.[300]

Lieutenant Colonel Benjamin Forsyth, the rugged tough rifle commander that played such an active role on the Upper St. Lawrence at the start of the war met his end in a skirmish along the Lower Canada frontier in June 1814.[301]

Arguably the best American commander of the war was Major General Jacob Brown, who in 1814 led the Left Division of the American army admirability in the invasion of the Niagara Peninsula. He was severally wounded at Lundy's Lane. When the war ended and the army was reduced, Brown was only one of two major generals kept. The other was Andrew Jackson. Despite financial problems after the war, Brown continued to buy and sell land till about 1820. He also continued in agriculture pursuits. In 1821, the army was reorganized in which Brown had been commanding the Northern Division. He now became the commanding general of the whole U.S. army. Just before taking command he suffered a stroke. When he had recovered enough, he headed to take charge of his new position. Brown died in 1828.[302]

David Parish, the wealthy banker who helped open up northern New York and finance the war for the U.S. government while at the same helping to supply the British with provisions, left for Europe in 1816. He soon became a partner in a Vienna commercial house, which the parties Parish became involved with lived a princely lifestyle. The firm went bankrupt and Parish soon lost much of his estates in Europe to pay his creditors.[303]

Despite the extreme importance of the St. Lawrence River to the survival of Upper Canada, the Americans made only one serious attempt to shut off the supply line. The British of course were very aware of this vulnerability and took steps to correct this in the period following the war. In the event of another war with the United States, the British began work on the Rideau Canal, which linked the Ottawa River with Bytown (modern Ottawa) to Kingston. The Rideau Canal was opened in 1832 which would now allow them to move supplies to Kingston without being exposed to American attack from the south side of the St. Lawrence River as they had been during the War of 1812.

Improvements were made for navigation along the Upper St. Lawrence which had hampered upriver shipping for years. In 1817 the canals at Cascades, Split Rock and Coteau-du-Lace were widened to 12 feet and deepened to 3 and a half feet. Work began in 1821 on the Lachine Canal to bypass the rapids there. Although the canal was for commercial use, the British government provided a large amount of the funding so as it would meet military requirements.

To bypass the Long Sault Rapids, work began on the Cornwall canal in 1834 but was halted due to financial trouble and the 1837-38 rebellions. In 1841, the heavily indebted Upper and Lower Canada were united and managed to get a loan of £1.5 million sterling from London for the improving and building of the canals along the St. Lawrence and new roads. Much of the motivation to improve and construct the St. Lawrence Canals was the completion of the Erie Canal in 1825 which was beginning to take a lot of business away form the merchants at Montreal. By 1848, the St. Lawrence Canals were complete. The almost 9 mile long Lachine Canal was improved. It now had five locks instead of the original seven. The locks were 200 feet long, 45 feet wide and 9 feet of water on the sills, which was the universal size for all the locks on the St. Lawrence. The little canals at Coteau-du-Lac, Split Rock and the Cascades were replaced by the over 11 mile long Beauharnois Canal which had nine locks. This canal was built on the south of the river. Work on the 11 mile Cornwall Canal began again being completed in 1842. It had six locks. The Williamsburg Canals, which actually consisted of three canals to bypass the rapids at Farran's Point, Rapid de Plat and Galops were all completed by 1847. There were six locks and combined the canals were over 12 miles long. Originally, the Galops canal were constructed in two sections: one a Cardinal and the other at Iroquois. They were united between 1849 to 1851.[304]

In 1958, the Upper St. Lawrence between Cornwall and Iroquois was changed forever with the opening of the St. Lawrence/Seaway. A joint project by Canada and the United States, the seaway now allowed ocean vessels to head up to the Great Lakes - the heart of the continent. As a result of the huge undertaking, the battle site of Crysler's Farm was submerged as 20,000 acres of land were flooded on the Canadian side of the river. Six neighboring villages, Milles Roches, Dickinson's Landing, Moulinette, Wales, Farran's Point and Aultsville would also be flooded. All of Iroquois was moved inland, while part of Morrisburg was to be submerged.

ENDNOTES

1.Richard Preston, *Kingston Before the War of 1812: A Collection of Documents* (Toronto: University of Toronto, 1959), 39; Hazel C. Mathews, *Frontier Spies: The British Secret Service, Northern Department during the Revolutionary War* (Fort Myers, Florida: Ace Press, Inc., 1971), 146.

2. David Jones is better known for being the fiance of Jane McRae who was killed by Indians during Burgoyne's campaign.

3.Christopher Moore, *The Loyalists: Revolution, Exile, Settlement* (Toronto: McClelland & Stewart Inc., 1984 additions to original edition: 1994), 179; Ernest Cruikshank,. *The King's Royal Regiment of New York* (Toronto: The Ontario Historical Society, 1931), 108.

4.The Iroquois in 1784 were made up six tribes: Mohawk, Oneidas, Onondagas, Cayugas, Senecas and Tuscaroras which joined the Iroquois league in the early 1720s. Peter D. MacLeod, *The Canadian Iroquois and the Seven Years' War* (Toronto: Dundurn Press, 1996), xi; Carl Benn, *The Iroquois in the War of 1812* (Toronto: University of Toronto, 1998), 15.

5.The Department of Transport, *The Canals of Canada* (Ottawa, 1946), 10.

6.George Heriot, *Travels through the Canadas* (London, 1807, reprinted by Edmonton: M.G. Hurtig Ltd, 1971), 125.

7.Normand Lafreniere, *Canal Building on the St. Lawrence River: Two Centuries of Works 1779 - 1959* (Ottawa: Parks Canada, 1983), 17-19; Jacob Farrand Pringle, *The Old Eastern District: Its Settlement and Early Progress* (Cornwall: S.I., 1890), 152.

8.Cruikshank, *The King's Royal Regiment of New York*, 111.

9.George A. Rawlyk, *"Loyalist Military Settlements in Upper Canada,,"* The *Loyal Americans: The Military Role of the Loyalist Provincial Corps and Their Settlements in British North America, 1775-1784* (Ottawa: National Museum of Canada, 1983), 101.

10.*ibid.*, 101-102.

11.Benn, *The Iroquois in the War of 1812*, 18-19.

12.Mathews, *Frontier Spies: The British Secret Service, Northern Department during the Revolutionary War*, 152; Pringle, *The Old Eastern District: Its Settlement and Early Progress*, 101-102.

13.There are legends, which may or may not be true, that in the late 1770s a small settlement of Loyalists settled around St. Andrews on the Raisin River, near Cornwall.

14.Gerald M. Craig, *Upper Canada: The Formative Years 1784-1841* (Toronto: McClelland and Stewart Limited, 1963), 5-6, 12; Elinor Kyte Senior, "The Loyalists in Cornwall 1784-1984," in *None was ever better . . . "The Loyalist Settlement of Ontario": Proceedings of the Annual Meeting of the Ontario Historical Society Cornwall, June 1984* (Stormont, Dundas and Glengarry Historical Society, July 1984), 3.

15.quoted from John Graham Harkness, *Stormont, Dundas and Glengarry: A History 1784-1945* Ottawa: Mutual Press Limited, 1946, reprinted 1972), 53.

16.Robert J. Burns, *Fort Wellington: A Narrative and Structural History, 1812-1838* (Ottawa: Parks Canada, 1979), 4; Senior, "The Loyalists in Cornwall 1784-1984," 5; Craig, *Upper Canada*, 11-12.

17.Agnes Maule Machar, *The Story of Old Kingston* (Toronto: The Musson Book Co.,1908), 82.

18.Preston, *Kingston Before the War of 1812*, lxxxi.

19.George Sheppard, *Plunder, Profit and Paroles: A Social History of the War of 1812 in Upper Canada* (Montreal: McGill-Queen's University Press, 1994)18-19; Burns, *Fort Wellington*, 5;
Craig, *Upper Canada*, 24.

20.Charles D. Anderson, *Bluebloods & Rednecks: Discord and Rebellion in the 1830s* (Burnstown, Ontario: General Store Publishing, 1996), 5-6; Harkness, *Stormont, Dundas and Glengarry*, 55; William Gray, *Soldiers of the King: The Upper Canadian Militia 1812-1815* (Erin, Ontario: The Boston Mills Press, 1995),17.

21.George Rawlyk and Janice Potter, "Richard Cartwright", *Dictionary of Canadian Biography* (www.biographi.ca), 1-2; Burns, *Fort Wellington*, 6.

22. D.E. Fitzpatrick, "William Gilkison", *Dictionary of Canadian Biography* (www.biographi.ca) 1.

23. Burns, *Fort Wellington*, 7-8.

24. Franklin B. Hough, *A History of St. Lawrence and Franklin Counties, New York from the Earliest Period to the Present Time* (Albany: Little & Co., 1853), 238, 253.

25. *Ibid.*, 371.

26. *Ibid.*, 371-372; Isabel Thompson Kelsay, *Joseph Brant 1743-1807: A Man of Two Worlds* (Syracuse, New York: Syracuse University Press, 1984), 373-374; Robert Allen, *His Majesty's Indian Allies: British Indian Policy in the Defence of Canada, 1774-1815* (Toronto: Dundurn Press, 1993), 57.

27. Hough, *A History of St. Lawrence and Franklin Counties*, 372.

28. *Ibid.*, 376.

29. Harry F. Landon, *Bugles on the Border* (Watertown, N.Y.: The Watertown Daily Times, 1954), 7.

30. Hough, *A History of St. Lawrence and Franklin Counties*, 407.

31. *Ibid.*, 600-603; Landon, *Bugles on the Border*, 7; Preston, *Kingston Before the War of 1812*, lxviii-lxxviii.

32. Preston, *Kingston Before the War of 1812*, 221-224.

33. *Ibid.*, 224-225.

34. *Ibid.*, 225-226.

35. quoted in Sandy Antal, *A Wampum Denied: Proctor's War of 1812* (Ottawa: Carleton University Press, 1997), 17.

36. Allen, *His Majesty's Indian Allies*, 116.

37. Donald Hickey, *The War of 1812: A Forgotten Conflict* (Chicago: University of Illinois Press, 1989), 10; Robin Reilly, *The British at the Gates: The New Orleans Campaign in the War of 1812* (Toronto: Robin Brass Studio, 2002 originally published by G.P Putnam's Sons, New York, 1974), 12-13, 19.

38. Hickey, *The War of 1812*, 11. Possibly as high as 6000 American sailors were impressed by the Royal Navy from 1803-1812.

39. *Ibid.*, 17. Four years later a similar incident happened when the U.S. frigate *President* traded fire with the Royal Navy's *Little Belt* with the British getting the worst of it suffering 30 casualties. There was some debate who fired first.

40. George Stanley, *The War of 1812: Land Operations* (Toronto: Macmillian of Canada (in collaboration with the National Museum of Man, National Museum of Canada, 1983), 18-19.

41. Hough, *A History of St. Lawrence and Franklin Counties*, 618; quoted in Landon, *Bugles on the Border*, 12.

42. Sackett to Cartwright, 9 August 1808, *Selected British Documents of the Canadian War of 1812*, 1:149; *Ibid.*, Mackenzie to Thornton, 24 August 1808, *Ibid.*, 1:150.

43. Preston, *Kingston Before the War of 1812*, lxxxvi.

44. Cartwright to McKenzie, 2 November 1808, *Selected British Documents of the Canadian War of 1812*, 1:157.

45. Cartwright to Gore, 5 November 1808, *Ibid.*, 1:158-159; Deposition of Andrew Denyke, 3 November 1808, *Ibid.*, 1:159-160; Deposition of John Fuston, 3 November 1812, *Ibid.*, 1:161:162.

46. Patrick Wilder, *The Battle of Sackett's Harbor 1813* (Baltimore: The Nautical & Aviation Publishing Company of America, 1994), 15.

47. Hickey, *The War of 1812*, 42.

48. Philip Katcher, *The American War 1812-1814 (*London: Osprey Publishing, 1990), 27.

49. quoted in Katcher, *The American War 1812-1814*, 3.

50. Brock to Prevost, 2 December 1811, *Selected British Documents of the Canadian War of 1812*, 1:276; Ernest A. Cruikshank, 'A Study of Disaffection in Upper Canada in 1812-15', *The Defended Border: Upper Canada and the War of 1812* (Morris Zaslow ed.) (Toronto: The Macmillian Company of Canada Limited, 1964 first appeared in the 'Transactions' of the Royal Society of Canada, series three, section 2, 1912), 206.

51. quoted in Wesley B.Turner, *British Generals in the War of 1812: High Command in the Canadas* (Montreal: McGill-Queen's University Press, 1999), 30.

52. Robert Malcomson, *Lords of the Lake: The Naval War on Lake Ontario, 1812-1814* (Toronto: Robin Brass Studio, 1998), 26-27; C.P. Stacey, 'The Defence of Upper Canada, 1812', *The Defended Border: Upper Canada and the War of 1812* (Morris Zaslow ed.) (Toronto: The Macmillian Company of Canada Limited, 1964 taken from 'Introduction to the Study of Military History for Canadian Students' 1960), 12-13.

53. Winston Johnston, *The Glengarry Light Infantry, 1812-1816: Who Were They and What Did They do in the war?* (Charlottetown, Benson Publishing, 1998), 31. Johnston has wrote a wonderful book on the Glengarrys clearing up many myths that surround this famous regiment.

54. *Ibid.*, 242.

55. Brock to Baynes, 29 July 1812, *Selected British Documents of the Canadian War of 1812*, 1:396; Sheppard, *Plunder, Profit and Paroles*, 15.

56. Brock to Baynes, 29 July 1812, *Selected British Documents of the Canadian War of 1812*, 1:397.

57. C.E. Cartwright, *Life and Letters of the Late Hon. Richard Cartwright* (Toronto: Belford Brothers, 1876), 96.

58. Gray, *Soldiers of the King*, 26.

59. An Act to extend the Provisions of an Act passed in the forty-eighth year of his Majesty's reign, intituled, "An Act to Explain, Amend and Reduce to one Act of Parliament the several Laws now in being for the Raising and Training the Militia of the Province", 6 March 1812, *Selected British Documents of the Canadian War of 1812,* 1:175, 183.

60. Colonel W. Boss and Brigadier General W. J. Patterson, *Up the Glens: Stormont, Dundas and Glengarry Highlanders 1783-1994* (Cornwall: The Old Book Store, 1995) 6; Stanely, *The War of 1812* 69-70.

61. William Dunlop, *William. Tiger Dunlop's Upper Canada: Comprising Recollections of the American Army 1812-1814 and Statistical Sketches of Upper Canada for the Use of Emigrants by a Backwoodsman* (Toronto: McClelland and Stewart Limited, 1967) 24.

62. Stanely, *War of 1812*, 71; Frank Mackey, *Steamboat Connection: Montreal to Upper Canada, 1816-1843* (Montreal & Kingston: McGill-Queen's University Press, 2000) 8.

63. Adjutant General's Office, 24 April 1812, *Selected British Documents of the Canadian War of 1812*, 1:300.

64. Head Quarters Montreal, 22 September 1812, *Ibid.*, 1:333.

65. Burns, *Fort Wellington*, 13-14.

66. Pringle, *The Old Eastern District*, 75.

67. John D. Morris, *Sword of the Border: Major General Jacob Jennings Brown 1775-1828* (Kent, Ohio: The Kent State University Press, 2000), 25; Quimby, Robert S., *The U.S. Army in the War of 1812: An Operational and Command Study* (2 Vols.; East Lansing, Michigan: Michigan State University Press, 1997), 1:2; Benson J. Lossing, *The Pictorial Field-Book of the War of 1812* (New York: Harper & Brothers, Publishers, 1869), 366.

68. Lossing, *The Pictorial Field-Book of the War of 1812*, 374-375.

69. *Ibid.*, 659-660; Major C.C.J. Bond, "The British Base at Carleton Island", *Ontario History* (Vol. LII No. 1 March 1960), 16; Wilder, *The Battle of Sackett's Harbor 1813*. 17.

70. Burns, *Fort Wellington*, 11-12.

71. Hough, *A History of St. Lawrence and Franklin Counties*, 621; Thad W. H. Leavitt, *History of Leeds & Greenville, Ontario from 1749 to 1879 with Illustrations and Biographical Sketches of Some of its Prominent Men and Pioneers* (Brockville: Recorder Press, 1879), 33.

72. Lighter than a long gun of the same caliber, a carronade was a short barreled, smooth bored ordnance. It also required a smaller crew to man it than a long gun, but a carronade had the disadvantage of having a third the range of a long gun of the same caliber.

73. Some sources put command of the brigade under Major Heathcote.

74. Robert Henderson, "Soldier's Families Under Fire: Ambush at Toussaint Island 1812", *The Discriminating General* (The War of 1812 Website www.militaryheritage.com/ambush.htm).

75. Croil, *Dundas*, 98-99; Hough, *A History of St. Lawrence and Franklin Counties*, 624; Mary Agnes FitzGibbon, *A Veteran of 1812: The Life of James FitzGibbon*. (Toronto: Propero Books, 2000 originally published by William Briggs, 1894), 64-65.

76. Some sources put the number at 70 riflemen and 34 militiamen.

77. The redcoated militiamen caused Forsyth to believe he was facing a combined force of regulars and militia.

78. Lossing, *The Pictorial Field Book of the War of 1812*, 372-373; J. Mackay Hitsman, *The Incredible War of 1812: A Military History* (Toronto: Robin Brass Studio, 1999 originally published by University of Toronto, 1965), 106-107.

79. Henry R. Dawson, *Battles of the United States, by Sea and Land: Embracing those of the Revolutionary and Indian Wars, The War of 1812 and The Mexican War* (New York: Johnson, Fry, and Company, 1858) 2:137-138; Morris, *Sword of the Border*, 29; Leavitt, *History of Leeds & Greenville*, 34; Hough, *A History of St. Lawrence and Franklin Counties*, 625.

80. Donald E. Graves editor, *Merry Hearts Make Light Days: The War of 1812 Journal of Lieutenant John Le Couteur, 104th Foot*, (Ottawa: Carleton University Press, 1993), 113.

81. Dunlop, *Tiger Dunlop's Upper Canada*, 27.

82. Baynes to Macdonell, 16 October 1812, in Ernest Cruikshank, ed., *The Documentary History of the Campaign upon the Niagara Frontier in the Year 1812* (Welland: Tribune Office, 1900), p. 4:133.

83. Dawson, *Battles of the United States*, 2:173-175.

84. Gray to Baynes, 23 November 1812, *Selected British Documents of the Canadian War of 1812*, 1:673.

85. *Ibid.*, 1:673.

86. *Ibid.*, 1:672-675; Johnston, *The Glengarry Light Infantry, 1812-1816*, 89-92; Benn, *The Iroquois in the War of 1812*, 62.

87. Malcomson, *Lords of the Lake*, 49; Lossing, *The Pictorial Field-Book of the War of 1812*, 371-371; Hitsman, *The Incredible War of 1812*, 110-112.

88. The King's German Legion was the largest and most effective foreign corps serving in the British army at the time. Many of the troops in the legion were from Hanover which had been overrun by the French in 1803. The Legion served in

Europe and it is unusual that De Gaugreben was sent to the Canadas.

89. Bruyeres to Prevost, 19 January 1813, *Selected British Documents of the Canadian War*, 2:64; Burns, *Fort Wellington*, 33.

90. Bruyeres to Prevost, 19 January 1813, *Selected British Documents of the Canadian War*, 2:64-68.

91. J. Smyth Carter, *The Story of Dundas: Being a History of the County of Dundas from 1784 to 1904* (Iroquois, Ontario: The St. Lawrence News Publishing, 1905 reprinted as Canadiana Reprint Series No. 9, Global Heritage Press, 1999), 245-246.

92. Leavitt, *History of Leeds and Greenville*, 40.

93. Stanely, *War of 1812*, 230.

94. Some accounts say a 6-pounder.

95. Hough, *A History of St. Lawrence and Franklin Counties*, 627-628.

96. Macdonell to Harvey, 25 February 1813, *Selected British Documents of the Canadian War of 1812*, 2:20-24; Edgar, *Ten Years of Upper Canada in Peace and War 1805-1815*, 176-177; Hough, *A History of St. Lawrence and Franklin Counties*, 629-630; Dawson, *Battles of the United States*, 2:203-205.

97. Hough, *A History of St. Lawrence and Franklin Counties*, 630-634; Morris, *Sword of the Border*, 37.

98. Macdonell to Harvey, 22 February 1813, *Selected British Documents of the Canadian War of 1812*, 2:16; Johnston, *The Glengarry Light Infantry, 1812-1816*, 229.

99. Macdonell to Harvey, 25 February 1813, *Selected British Documents of the Canadian War of 1812*, 2:24; Kingston Gazette, March 23 1813, Nova Scotia Royal Gazette, March 1813, in Johnston, *The Glengarry Light Infantry, 1812-1816*, 106.

100. Hough, *A History of St. Lawrence and Franklin Counties*, 634.

101. quoted in Hitsman, *The Incredible War of 1812*, 133.

102. quoted in Stanely, *War of 1812*, 231-232.

103. Boss and Patterson, *Up the Glens*, 7; Gray, *Soldiers of the King*, 187-189; Burns, *Fort Wellington*, 46-47; C.J. Shepard, "Richard Duncan Fraser", *Dictionary of Canadian Biography*. (www.biographi.ca), 1.

104. Baynes, 8 April 1813, *Selected British Documents of the Canadian War of 1812*, 3:673-674; Stanley, *War of 1812*, 71.

105. John Grodzinski, "Command Structure and Appointments in Upper Canada, 1812-1814", *The War of 1812 Magazine* (Issue 1: January 2006, www.napolean-series.org), 4.

106. Graves, *Merry Hearts Make Light Days*, 93-103; Baynes, 27 March 1813, *Selected British Documents of the Canadian War of 1812*, 2:79-80.

107. Baynes, 20 March 1813, *Selected British Documents of the Canadian War of 1812*, 2:78-79.

108. General Orders, Baynes, 19 May 1813, *Ibid.*, 2:120-122.

109. quoted in Machar, *The Story of Old Kingston*, 118-121.

110. *Ibid.*, 123.

111. quoted in Henry Adams, *The War of 1812* (New York: Cooper Square Press, 1999) 77.

112. *Ibid.*, 80-82.

113. Stacy was detained by Chauncey who wrote on July 4, 1813 to the Secretary of the Navy, that he could prove the man "frequent intercourse with the enemy". Chauncey thought it would be a good idea to hang Stacy as a warning to other Americans spying for the British.

114. Commander Robert Barclay was briefly in command before Yeo. He arrived at Kingston with a handful others naval personnel a few weeks before Yeo and the bulk of the naval contingent.

115. Wilder, *The Battle of Sackett's Harbour 1813*, 69-70; Hitsman, *The Incredible War of 1812*, 118; Prevost to Bathurst, 1 June 1813, *Selected British Documents of the Canadian War of 1812*, 2:130.

116. *Ibid.*, 2:130-131.

117. Baynes to Prevost, 30 May 1813, *Ibid.*, 123.

118. Malcomson, *Lords of the Lake.*, 130; Prevost to Bathurst, 1 June 1813, *Selected British Documents of the Canadian War of 1812*, 2:131.

119. Morris, *Sword of the Border*, 40.

120. Graves, *Merry Hearts Make Light Days*, 115.

121. Wilder, *The Battle of Sackett's Harbour 1813*, 75.

122. *Ibid.*, 78.

123. quoted in Stanley, *War of 1812*, 235.

124. Baynes to Prevost, 30 May 1813, *Selected British Documents of the Canadian War of 1812*, 2:124.

125. quoted in Morris, *Sword of the Border*, 45.

126. Baynes to Prevost, 30 May 1813, *Selected British Documents of the Canadian War of 1812*, 2:124.

127. Wilder, *The Battle of Sackett's Harbour 1813*, 90; Dawson, *Battles of the United States*, 2:238; Quimby, *The U.S. Army in the War of 1812*, 1:238; Baynes to Prevost, 30 May 1813, *Selected British Documents of the Canadian War of 1812*, 2:124.

128. Graves, *Merry Hearts Make Light Days*, 116. In August 1814 his luck ran out when he was killed in an assault on the American held Fort Erie.

129. Baynes to Prevost, 30 May 1813, *Selected British Documents of the Canadian War of 1812*, 2:124-125.

130. Morris, *Sword of the Border*, 45-46; Baynes to Prevost, 30 May 1813, *Selected British Documents of the Canadian War of 1812*, 2:125; Dawson, *Battles of the United States*, 2:238.

131. Wilder, *The Battle of Sackett's Harbour 1813*, 98, 102.

132. Graves, *Merry Hearts Make Light Days*, 117.

133. Baynes to Prevost, 30 May 1813, *Selected British Documents of the Canadian War of 1812*, 2:125.

134. Chauncey later claimed he had raised the flag to distinguish his ship from the that of the Royal Navy. He also said he could not remember giving Drury order to burn the naval stores and building on the signal of lowering the red flag.

135. Baynes to Prevost, 30 May 1813, *Selected British Documents of the Canadian War of 1812* 2:126.

136. quoted in Wilder, *The Battle of Sackett's Harbour 1813*, 110.

137. Graves, *Merry Hearts Make Light Days*, 117.

138. Prevost to Bathurst, 1 June 1813, *Selected British Documents of the Canadian War of 1812*, 2:132, 134.

139. Turner, *British General in the War of 1812*, 102-103.

140. Adam Norman Lynde, "The War from the Saddle: The Diary of Lieutenant John Lang, 19th Light Dragoons" *The Discriminating General: The War of 1812 Website* (www.militaryheritage.ca/lang.htm), 7-8; Baynes, 20 June 1813, *Selected British Documents of the Canadian War of 1812*, 2:157.

141. Adam Norman Lynde, "The War from the Saddle: The Diary of Lieutenant John Lang, 19th Light Dragoons. Part Two", *The Discriminating General: The War of 1812 Website* (www.militaryheritage.ca/lang2.htm), 6.

142. Burns, *Fort Wellington*, 19-20.

143. Buffalo Gazette, 10 August 1813, *The Documentary History of the Campaign upon the Niagara Frontier*, 6:288.

144. Baynes, 24 July 1813, *Ibid.*, 2:271-273; Buffalo Gazette, 10 August 1813, *Ibid.*, 6:288-289.

145. Yeo to Prevost, 21 July 1813, *Selected British Documents of the Canadian War of 1812*, 2:429.

146. Pearson to Prevost, 9 August 1813, *Ibid.*, 2:430; Hitsman, *The Incredible War of 1812*, 177-178..

147. Pearson to Baynes, 22 August 1813, *Selected British Documents of the Canadian War of 1812*, 2:433-434.

148. Dale Van Every, *Ark of Empire: The American Frontier 1784-1803* (New York: William Morrow, 1963), 117-118; John S.D. Eisenhower, *Agent of Destiny: The Life and Times of General Winfield Scott* (Norman: University of Oklahoma,

1997), 15.

149. Ibid., 66; Adams, *The War of 1812*, 91.

150. Secretary of War to Wilkinson, 8 August 1813, *The Documentary History of the Campaign upon the Niagara Frontier*, 6:322-323.

151. Minutes of Council of War Holden at Sackett's Harbor, 26 August 1813, *ibid.*, 7:73-74.

152. J.K. Johnson, "William Johnston", *Dictionary of Canadian Biography* (www.biographi.ca), 1.

153. Wilkinson to Brown, 29 August 1813, *The Documentary History of the Campaign upon the Niagara Frontier*, 7:85-86.

154. Secretary of War to Wilkinson, 6 September 1813, *Ibid.*, 7:106.

155. Secretary of War to Wilkinson, 22 September 1813, *Ibid.*, 7:163.

156. Wilkinson to Secretary of War, 27 September, *Ibid.*, 7:168; Lewis to Mrs. Lewis, 3 October 1813, *Ibid.*, 7:191.

157. quoted in Adams, *The War of 1812*, 93.

158. *Ibid.*, 96.

159. Wilkinson to Chauncey, 9 October 1813, *The Documentary History of the Campaign upon the Niagara Frontier*, 7:217; Chauncey toWilkinson, 9 October 1813, *Ibid.*, 7:217.

160. General Order, 9 October 1813, *Ibid.*, 7:217-218; Donald E. Graves, *Field of Glory: The Battle of Crysler's Farm, 1813* (Toronto: Robin Brass Studio, 1999),.356.

161. Quimby, *The U.S. Army in the War of 1812*, 1:335.

162. Wilkinson to the Secretary of War, 18 October 1813, *The Documentary History of the Campaign upon the Niagara Frontier*, 8:77.

163. Secretary of War to Wilkinson, 19 October 1813, *Ibid.*, 8:81-82; Adams, *The War of 1812*, 97.

164. Secretary of War to Wilkinson, 20 October 1813, *The Documentary History of the Campaign upon the Niagara Frontier*, 8:85.

165. Extract of a Letter from an Officer in the Army, 26 October 1813, *Ibid.*, 8:95.

166. Chauncey to Secretary Navy, 30 October 1813, *Ibid.*, 8:106.

167. Pearson to Baynes, 12 October 1813, *Selected British Documents of the Canadian War of 1812*, 2:434-435.

168. Hough, *A History of St. Lawrence and Franklin Counties*, 635.

169. Pearson to Baynes, 17 October 1813, *The Documentary History of the Campaign upon the Niagara Frontier*, 8:73.

170. This man probably was Samuel Casey.

171. Information from Sackett's Harbour received at Kingston, 17 October 1813, *The Documentary History of the Campaign upon the Niagara Frontier*, 8:74.

172. Vincent to Rottenburg, 18 October 1813, *Ibid.*, 78; Rottenburg to Prevost, 18 October 1813, 8:79; Petition of Samuel Casey, *Ibid.*, 8:116; Rottenburg to Prevost, 15 October 1813, *Selected British Documents of the Canadian War of 1812*, 2:214; Yeo to Prevost, 17 October 1813, *Ibid.*, 2:215-216.

173. Baynes, 7 November 1813, *Selected British Documents of the Canadian War of 1812*, 2:437.

174. Secretary of War to Hampton, 16 October 1813, *The Documentary History of the Campaign upon the Niagara Frontier*, 8:70-71.

175. An abatis is an obstacle created by fallen trees with the branches facing outward.

176. Hitsman, *The Incredible War of 1812*, 181, 184; Quimby, *The U.S. Army in the War of 1812*, 1:327-328.

177. Allan S. Everest, *The War of 1812 in the Champlain Valley* (Syracuse, New York: Syracuse University Press, 1981), 130-133; P.G. Smith, "Birth of the Canadian Army" *Military History* (Volume 20 Number 4. Leesburg, Va.: Primedia Inc, October, 2003), 55-56; Hitsman, *The Incredible War of 1812*, 186-187; Hough, *A History of St. Lawrence and Franklin Counties*, 653; Quimby, *The U.S. Army in the War of 1812*, 1:328-330; Hampton to the Secretary of War, 1 November 1813, *The Documentary History of the Campaign upon the Niagara Frontier*, 8:122-123.

178. Hough, *A History of St. Lawrence and Franklin Counties*, 641-642; Croil, *Dundas*, 99.

179. *Ibid.*, 100-101.

180. Kingston Gazette, 6 November 1813, *The Documentary History of the Campaign upon the Niagara Frontier*, 8:138.

181. Mulcaster to Yeo, 2 November 1812, *Ibid.*, 123-124; Brown to Dennis, 2 November 1813, *Ibid.*, 8:126.

182. Lewis to Mrs. Lewis, 2 November 1813, *Ibid.*, 123, Wilkinson to the Secretary of the War, 3 November 1813, *Ibid.*, 8:126.

183. Journal Referred to in the Foregoing Letter of Major General Wilkinson, *Ibid.*, 8:212.

184. *Ibid.*, 8:212.

185. Dennis to Scott, 11 November 1813, *Ibid.*, 8:155-156.

186. Journal Referred to in the Foregoing Letter of Major General Wilkinson, *Ibid.*, 8:212-213; Hough, *A History of St. Lawrence and Franklin Counties*,. 639.

187. Wilkinson, 6 November 1813, *Selected British Documents of the Canadian War of 1812*, 2:441.

188. Wilkinson to Hampton, 6 November 1813, *The Documentary History of the Campaign upon the Niagara Frontier*, 8:140-141; Journal Referred to in the Foregoing Letter of Major General Wilkinson, *Ibid.*, 8:213.

189. Croil, *Dundas*, 78.

190. C.J. Shepard, "Richard Duncan Fraser", 1; Boss and Patterson, *Up the Glens*, 12-13; Burns, *Fort Wellington*, 53.

191. Journal Referred to in the Foregoing Letter of Major General Wilkinson, *The Documentary History of the Campaign upon the Niagara Frontier*, 8:213.

192. *Ibid.*, 214.

193. Croil, *Dundas*, 78-79.

194. Journal Referred to in the Foregoing Letter of Major General Wilkinson, *The Documentary History of the Campaign upon the Niagara Frontier*, 8:214.

195. *Ibid.*, 8:214.

196. Council of War at the White House Near Hamilton on the St. Lawrence, 8 November 1813, *Ibid.*, 8:145.

197. MacMahon to Powell, 8 November 1813, *Ibid.*, 8:143.

198. quoted in Ronald Way, "The Day of Crysler's Farm", *The Defended Border: Upper Canada and the War of 1812* Morris Zaslow ed., (Toronto: The Macmillian Company of Canada Limited, 1964 first appeared in 'Canadian Geographical Journal' Vol 62, June 1962), 65-66; Carl Christie, "Joseph Wanton Morrison", *Dictionary of Canadian Biography* (www.biographi.ca) 1.

199. Phillip Buckner, "Sir John Harvey", *Ibid.*, 1.

200. Way, "The Day of Crysler's Farm", 65-66; Hitsman, *The Incredible War of 1812*, 188-189.

201. .Morrison's command may well have numbered around 1,200 men. I have chosen to put their strength at 800 rank and file because this is the number both Morrison and Harvey give in their reports of the battle of Crysler's Farm.

202. Journal Referred to in the Foregoing Letter of Major General Wilkinson, *The Documentary History of the Campaign upon the Niagara Frontier*, 8:214-215.

203. C.J. Shepard, "John Crysler", *Dictionary of Canadian Biography* (www.biographi.ca) 1.

204. .Morrison to Rottenburg, 11 November 1813, *Selected British Documents of the Canadian War of 1812*, 2:439-440; Hough, *A History of St. Lawrence and Franklin Counties*, 642.

205. Carter, *The Story of Dundas*, 238.

206. .Morning General Orders, 10 November 1813, *The Documentary History of the Campaign upon the Niagara Frontier*, 8:148.

207. Journal Referred to in the Foregoing Letter of Major General Wilkinson, *Ibid.*, 8:215-216; Way, "The Day of Crysler's Farm", 68.

208. Dennis to Scott, 10 November 1813, *The Documentary History of the Campaign upon the Niagara Frontier*, 8:150-151.

209. Cochrane to Scott, 11 November 1813, *Ibid.*, 8:152-153; Scott to Prevost, 11 November 1813, *Ibid.*, 8:153-154; Dennis to Scott, 11 November 1813, *Ibid.*, 8:154-155.

210. Croil, *Dundas*, 79, 81, 95; Carter, *The Story of Dundas*, 236-237.

211. MacMahon to Powell, 8 November 1813, *The Documentary History of the Campaign upon the Niagara Frontier*, 8:144; Croil, *Dundas*, 83.

212. Cochrane to Scott, 11 November 1813, *The Documentary History of the Campaign upon the Niagara Frontier*, 8:152; Pringle, *The Old Eastern District*, 77.

213. Wilkinson to the Secretary of War, 16 November 1813, *The Documentary History of the Campaign upon the Niagara Frontier*, 8:208.

214. Croil, *Dundas*, 84; Way, "The Day of Crysler's Farm", 73.

215. Wilkinson to the Secretary of War, 16 November 1813, *The Documentary History of the Campaign upon the Niagara Frontier*, 8:208-209; Boyd to Wilkinson, 12 November 1813, *Ibid.*, 8:170-171.

216. Carter, *The Story of Dundas*, 238.

217. Boyd to Wilkinson, 12 November 1813, *The Documentary History of the Campaign upon the Niagara Frontier*, 8:171; Morrison to Rottenburg, 12 November 1813, *Selected British Documents of the Canadian War of 1812*, 2:442; Hough, *A History of the St. Lawrence and Franklin Counties*, 647.

218. Boyd to Wilkinson, 12 November 1813, *The Documentary History of the Campaign upon the Niagara Frontier*, 8:171

219. Morrison to Rottenburg, 12 November 1813, *Selected British Documents of the Canadian War of 1812*, 2:442; Edgar, *Ten Years of Upper Canada in Peace and War, 1805-1815*, 252.

220. Hough, *A History of St. Lawrence and Franklin Counties*, 647; Edgar, *Ten Years of Upper Canada in Peace and War, 1805-1815*, 252; Boyd to Wilkinson, 12 November 1813, *The Documentary History of the Campaign upon the Niagara Frontier*, 8:171.

221. quoted in Way, "The Day of Crysler's Farm", 76.

222. *Ibid.*, 77; Edgar, *Ten Years of Upper Canada in Peace and War, 1805-1815*, 253; Morrison to Rottenburg, 12 November 1813, *Selected British Documents of the Canadian War of 1812*, 2:442.

223. quoted in Way, "The Day of Crysler's Farm", 76.

224. Boyd to Wilkinson, 12 November 1813, *The Documentary History of the Campaign upon the Niagara Frontier*, 8:172.

225. .Morrison to Rottenburg, 12 November 1813, *Selected British Documents of the Canadian War of 1812*, 442.

226. Hough, *A History of St. Lawrence and Franklin Counties*, 648; Dawson, *Battles of the United States*, 2:308.

227. .Morrison to Rottenburg, 12 November 1813, *Selected British Documents of the Canadian War of 1812*, 2:442; Graves, *Field of Glory*, 239.

228. Edgar, *Ten Years of Upper Canada in Peace and War, 1805-1815*, 253; Morrison to Rottenburg, 12 November 1813, *Selected British Documents of the Canadian War of 1812*, 2:442.

229. Way, "The Day of Crysler's Farm", 78-79.

230. *Ibid.*, 79; Morrison to Rottenburg, 12 November 1813, *Selected British Documents of the Canadian War of 1812*, 2:442-443; Hough, *A History of St. Lawrence and Franklin Counties*, 648.

231. Boyd to Wilkinson, 12 November 1813, *The Documentary History of the Campaign upon the Niagara Frontier*, 8:172; Edgar, *Ten Years in Upper Canada in Peace and War, 1805-1815*, 253; Morrison to Rottenburg, 12 November 1813, *Selected British Documents of the Canadian War of 1812*, 2:443.

232. Croil, *Dundas*, 87; Hough, *A History of St. Lawrence and Franklin Counties*, 648.

233. Boyd to Wilkinson, 12 November 1813, *The Documentary History of the Campaign upon the Niagara Frontier*, 8:173, Return-Action at Williamsburg, 14 November 1813, *Ibid.*, 8:197; Way, "The Day of Crysler's Farm", 80.

234. Croil, *Dundas*, 87-88; Edgar, *Ten Years of Upper Canada in Peace and War, 1805-1815*, 250; Lewis to Mrs. Lewis, 13 November 1813, *The Documentary History of the Campaign upon the Niagara Frontier*, 8:175.

235. 'Granny' Mary Hoople had been captured as a young girl by the Delaware Indians in the late 1770s. She spent seven years with them before being released. She settled near Long Sault on the St. Lawrence River where she had a relative. She eventually married Henry Hoople and would have 12 children. Utilizing medicinal skills she learnt from the Indians, Mary helped heal many of the local settlers around her if they got sick.

236. Dunlop, *Tiger Dunlop's Upper Canada*, 15-16; Pringle, *The Old Eastern District*, 79.

237. Claus to Claus Jr., 11 May 1814, *The Documentary History of the Campaign upon the Niagara Frontier*, 8:167.

240. Edgar, *Ten Years of Upper Canada in Peace and War, 1805-1815*, 254.

241. Croil, *Dundas*, 94-96.

242. .Morrison to Baynes, 15 November 1813, *The Documentary History of the Campaign upon the Niagara Frontier*, 8:196.

241. Harvey to Baynes, 16 November 1813, *Ibid.*, 206.

242. .Morris, *Sword of the Border*, 68; Hough, *A History of St. Lawrence and Franklin Counties*, 648-649.

243. Quimby, *The U.S. Army in the War of 1812*, 1:347; Morris, *Sword of the Border*, 68; Mulcaster to Yeo, 20 December 1813, *The Documentary History of the Campaign upon the Niagara Frontier*, 9:29

244. *Ibid.*, 9:29.

245. .Morris, *Sword of the Border*, 70-72; Landon, *Bugles on the Border*, 54.

246. Harvey to Baynes, 16 November 1813, *The Documentary History of the Campaign upon the Niagara Frontier*, 8:205-206.

247. General Order, 13 February 1814, *Ibid.*, 9:176-177; Hough, *A History of St. Lawrence and Franklin Counties*, 642.

248. Croil, *Dundas*, 102-103; Hough, *A History of St. Lawrence and Franklin Counties*, 651; Baynes, 29 May 1814, *Selected British Documents of the Canadian War of 1812*, 3:7-9; Scott to Prevost, 7 June 1814, *Ibid.*, 3:8-9.

249. Baynes, 29 May 1814, *Selected British Documents of the Canadian War of 1812*, 3:7.) p. 7.

250. Izard to the Secretary of War, 31 July 1814, *The Documentary History of the Campaign upon the Niagara Frontier*, 1:115; Shepard, *Plunder, Profit and Paroles*, 116, 155; Burns, *Fort Weillington*, 42.

251. Edgar, *Ten Years of Upper Canada in Peace and War, 1805-1815*, 269.

252. Dunlop, *Tiger Dunlop's Upper Canada*, 22-23.

253. Edgar, *Ten Years of Upper Canada in Peace and War, 1805-1815*, 282.

254. quoted in Landon, *Bugles on the Border*, 34.

255. quoted in Landon, *Bugles on the Border*, 35.

256. Edgar, *Ten Years of Upper Canada in Peace and War*, 273.

257. Izard to the Secretary of War, 31 July 1814, *The Documentary History of the Campaign upon the Niagara Frontier*, 1:114-115.

258. *Ibid.*, 115.

259. Burns, *Fort Wellington*, 39.

260. Sheppard, *Plunder, Profit and Paroles*, 116, 156; William M. Weekes, 'The War of 1812: Civil Authority and Martial Law in Upper Canada', *The Defended Border: Upper Canada and the War of 1812* (Morris Zaslow ed.) (Toronto: The Macmillian Company of Canada Limited, 1964, first appeared in 'Ontario History' Vol. 48 Autumn 1956), 200.

261. Turner, *British Generals in the War of 1812*, 115; Drummond to Bathurst, 5 April 1814; *The Documentary History of the Campaign upon the Niagara Frontier*, 9:279.

262. Sheppard, *Plunder, Profit and Paroles*, 156-157.

263. Drummond to Bathurst, 5 April 1814, *The Documentary History of the Campaign upon the Niagara Frontier*, 9:279-280.

264. Pringle, *The Old Eastern District*, 79-80.

265. Burns, *Fort Wellington*, 42-43.

266. *Ibid.*, 51-56.

267. Gray, *Soldiers of the King*, 27-29, 41-42; Sheppard, *Plunder, Profit and Paroles*, 89; Weekes, 'The War of 1812: Civil Authority and Martial Law in Upper Canada', 193.

268. .Militia General Orders, 11 December 1813, *The Documentary History of the Campaign upon the Niagara Frontier*, 8:269.

269. An Act to prevent Desertion from his Majesty's Regular Forces, 6 March 1812, *Selected British Documents of the Canadian War of 1812*, 1:172.

271. Drummond to Prevost, 5 April 1814, *Selected British Documents of the Canadian War of 1812*, 3:42-43; Hitsman, *The Incredible War of 1812*, 202.

272. Drummond to Prevost, 2 April 1814, *Selected British Documents of the Canadian War of 1812*, 3:40-41; Yeo to Prevost, 13 April 1814, *Ibid.*, 3:44-45.

273. Prevost to Drummond, 30 April 1814, *Ibid.*, 3:49-50.

274. Drummond to Prevost, 3 May 1814, *The Documentary History of the Campaign upon the Niagara Frontier*, 9:323-324.

275. Stovia to Prevost, 5 May 1814, *Ibid.*, 9:329; Drummond to Prevost, 7 May 1814, *Selected British Documents of the Canadian War of 1812*, 3:52-53.

276. Quimby, *The U.S. Army in the War of 1812*, 2:507-508; Lossing, *The Pictorial Field-Book of the War of 1812*, 794-795.

277. Drummond to Prevost, 7 May 1814, *Selected British Documents of the Canadian War of 1812*, 3:53; Dawson, *Battles of the United States*, 2:340.

278. C. Winston-Clare, 'A Shipbuilder's War', *The Defended Border: Upper Canada and the War of 1812* (Morris Zaslow ed.) (Toronto: The Macmillian Company of Canada Limited, 1964 first appeared in 'The Mariner's Mirror'. Vol. 29, 1943), 169.

279. "New York Evening Post", 19 May 1814, *The Documentary History of the Campaign upon the Niagara Frontier*, 3:344; Drummond to Prevost, 7 May 1814, *Selected British Documents of the Canadian War of 1812*, 3:53-54.

280. *Ibid.*, 54; Johnston, *The Glengarry Light Infantry, 1812-1816*, 139-140.

281. Drummond to Prevost, 7 May 1814, *Selected British Documents of the Canadian War of 1812*, 3:54; Yeo to Croker, 9 May 1814, *Ibid.*, 3:62; "New York Evening Post", 19 May 1814, *The Documentary History of the Campaign upon the Niagara Frontier*, 3:344; Quimby. *The U.S. Army in the War of 1812*, 2:508.

282. Return of Killed and Wounded of the Troops, 6 May 1814, *Selected British Documents of the Canadian War of 1812*, 3:59; Landon, *Bugles on the Border*, 58.

283. Return of Ordnance & Ordnance Stores, 7 May 1814, *Selected British Documents of the Canadian War of 1812*, 3:59-60; Dawson, *Battles of the United States*, 2:342.

284. Drummond to Prevost, 14 May 1814, *Selected British Documents of the Canadian War of 1812*, 3:67; Secret Intelligence received from Lt Col Morrison, *Ibid.*, 3:68; Report of Information, 14 May 1814, *Ibid.*, 3:70.

285. Drummond to Prevost, 2 June 1814, *Ibid.*, 3:73; Dawson, *Battles of the United States*, 2:343.

286. Drummond to Prevost, 2 June 1814, *Selected British Documents of the Canadian War of 1812*, 3:73.

287. Dawson, *Battles of the United States*, 2:343-344; Quimby, *The U.S. Army in the War of 1812*, 2:510-511; Drummond to Prevost, 2 June 1814, *Selected British Documents of the Canadian War of 1812*, 3:74.

288. Edgar, *Ten Years of Upper Canada in Peace and War, 1805-1815,* 279.

289. Drummond to Prevost, 21 June 1814, *Selected British Documents of the Canadian War of 1812*, 3:80; Drummond to Prevost, 23 June 1814, *Ibid.*, 81.

290. Hough, *A History of St. Lawrence and Franklin Counties*, 655.

291. Burns, *Fort Wellington*, 21-24.

292. Hickey, *The War of 1812: A Forgotten Conflict*, 298.

293. *Ibid.*, 296.

294. Shepard, "John Crysler", 1-2.

295. *Ibid.*, 1; Boss and Patterson, *Up the Glens*, 12-13.

296. Sheppard, "Richard Duncan Fraser", 2.

297. Johnson, "William Johnston", 1.

298. Christie, "Joseph Wanton Morrison", 1-2.

299. Johnston, *The Glengarry Light Infantry*, 242-244.

300. Graves, *Field of Glory*, 314, 321.

301. Quimby, *The U.S. Army in the War of 1812*, 2:603.

302. Morris, *Sword of the Border*, 171-172, 181, 218.

303. Hough, *A History of St. Lawrence and Franklin Counties*, 604.

304. Lafreniere, *Canal Building on the St. Lawrence River*, 21-27; Donald Creighton, *The Empire of the St. Lawrence* (Toronto: The Macmillian Company of Canada Limited, 1970 originally published in 1956), 343.

BIBLIOGRAPHY

PRINTED DOCUMENTS

Cartwright, C.E., ed. *Life and Letters of the Late Hon. Richard Cartwright.* Toronto: Belford Brothers, 1876.

Cruikshank, Ernest, ed. *The Documentary History of the Campaign upon the Niagara Frontier.* 9 Vols. Welland, Ontario: Tribune Office for the Lundy's Lane Historical Society, 1899-1908.

Dunlop, William. *Tiger Dunlop's Upper Canada: Comprising Recollections of the American War 1812-1814 and Statistical Sketches of Upper Canada for the Use of Emigrants by a Backwoodsman.* Toronto: McClelland and Stewart Limited, 1967.

Edgar, Matilda. *Ten Years of Upper Canada in Peace and War 1805-1815: Being the Ridout Letters with Annotations.* Toronto: William Briggs, 1890.

Graves, Donald E., ed. *Merry Hearts Make Light Days: The War of 1812 Journal of Lieutenant John Le Couteur, 104th Regiment of Foot.* Ottawa: Carleton University Press, 1994.

Graves, Donald E. *Soldiers of 1814: American Enlisted Men's Memoirs of the Niagara Campaign.* Youngstown, New York: Old Fort Niagara Association, Inc., 1995.

Heriot, George. *Travels through the Canadas.* Edmonton: M.G. Hurtig Ltd., 1971 (first published by Charles E. Tuttle Company Inc.).

Preston, Richard, ed. *Kingston Before the War of 1812: A Collection of Documents.* Toronto: University of Toronto, 1959.

Wood, William, ed. *Selected British Documents of the Canadian War of 1812.* 3 Vols. Toronto: Champlain Society, 1920-1928.

SECONDARY WORKS

Adams, Henry. *The War of 1812*. New York: Cooper Square Press, 1999 (first published in 1944 consisting of chapters in *History of the United States during the Administration of Jefferson and Madison* 9 Vols. 1889-1891).

Allen, Robert. *His Majesty's Indian Allies: British Indian Policy in the Defence of Canada, 1774-1815*. Toronto: Dundurn Press, 1993.

Anderson, Charles D. *Bluebloods & Rednecks: Discord and Rebellion in the 1830s*. Burnstown, Ontario: General Store Publishing, 1996.

Antal, Sandy. *A Wampum Denied: Proctor's War of 1812*. Ottawa: Carleton University Press, 1997.

Benn, Carl. *The Iroquois in the War of 1812*. Toronto: University of Toronto, 1998.

Boss, Colonel W. and Brigadier General W. J. Patterson. *Up the Glens: Stormont, Dundas and Glengarry Highlanders 1783-1994*. Cornwall: The Old Book Store, 1995.

Burns, Robert J. *Fort Wellington: A Narrative and Structural History, 1812-1838*. Ottawa: Parks Canada, 1979.

Carter, J. Smyth. *The Story of Dundas: Being a History of the County of Dundas from 1784 to 1904*. Iroquois, Ontario: The St. Lawrence News Publishing, 1905 (reprinted as Canadiana Reprint Series No. 9, Global Heritage Press, 1999).

Craig, Gerald M. *Upper Canada: The Formative Years 1784-1841*. Toronto: McClelland and Stewart Limited, 1963.

Creighton, Donald. *The Empire of the St. Lawrence*. Toronto: The Macmillian Company of Canada Limited, 1970 (originally published in 1956).

Croil, James. *Dundas or A Sketch of Canadian History*. Belleville, Ontario: Mika Silk Screening Limited, 1972 (first published by B. Dawson & Son in 1861).

Cruikshank, Ernest A. *The King's Royal Regiment of New York*. Toronto: The Ontario Historical Society, 1931 (reprinted 1984 with Index, Appendices and a Master Muster Roll prepared by Gavin Watts, ed.).

Dawson, Henry R. *Battles of the United States, by Sea and Land: Embracing those of the Revolutionary and Indian Wars, The War of 1812 and The Mexican War Volume 2*. New York: Johnson, Fry, and Company, 1858.

Eisenhower, John S.D. *Agent of Destiny: The Life and Times of General Winfield*

Scott. Norman, Oklahoma: University of Oklahoma, 1997.

Everest, Allan S. *The War of 1812 in the Champlain Valley*. Syracuse. New York: Syracuse University Press, 1981.

FitzGibbon, Mary Agnes. *A Veteran of 1812: The Life and Times of James FitzGibbon*. Toronto: Propero Books, 2002 (first published by William Briggs in 1894).

Fryer, Mary Beacock and Christopher Dracott. *John Graves Simcoe 1752-1806: A Biography*. Toronto: Dundurn Press, 1998.

Graves, Donald E. *Field of Glory: The Battle of Crysler's Farm, 1813*. Toronto: Robin Brass Studio, 1999.

Gray, William. *Soldiers of the King: The Upper Canadian Militia 1812-1815: A Reference Guide*. Erin, Ontario: Boston Mills Press, 1995.

Guillet, Edwin C. *Pioneer Days in Upper Canada*. Toronto: University of Toronto Press, 1933 (reprinted 1979).

Harkness, John Graham. *Stormont, Dundas and Glengarry: A History 1784-1945*. Ottawa: Mutual Press Limited, 1946 reprinted 1972.

Haythornthwaite, Philip J. *Weapons & Equipment of the Napoleonic Wars*. London: Arms & Armour, 1996 (first published by Blandford Press in 1979).

Hickey, Donald. *The War of 1812: A Forgotten Conflict*. Chicago: University of Illinois Press, 1989.

Hitsman, J. Mackay. *The Incredible War of 1812: A Military History*. Toronto: Robin Brass Studio, 1999 (first published by University of Toronto, 1965).

Holmes, Richard. *Redcoat: The British Soldier in the Age of Horse and Musket*. London: HarperCollins Publishers, 2001.

Hough, Franklin. *A History of St. Lawrence and Franklin Counties, New York from the Earliest Period to the Present Time*. Albany: Little & Co., 1853.

Johnston, Winston. *The Glengarry Light Infantry, 1812-1816: Who Were They and What They Did in the War?*. Charlottetown: Benson Publishing, 1998.

Katcher, Philip. *The American War 1812-1814*. London: Osprey Publishing Ltd, 1990.

Kelsay, Isabel Thompson. *Joseph Brant 1743-1807: A Man of Two Worlds*. Syracuse, New York: Syracuse University Pres, 1984.

Lafreniere, Normand. *Canal Building on the St. Lawrence River: Two Centuries of Works 1779-1959*. Ottawa: Parks Canada, 1983.

Landon, Harry F. *Bugles on the Border*. Watertown, New York: The Watertown Daily Times, 1954.

Leavitt, Thad W.H. *History of Leeds & Grenville, Ontario from 1749 to 1879 with Illustratins and Biographical Sketches of Some of its Prominent Men and Pioneers*. Brockville: Recorder Press, 1879.

Lossing, Benson. *The Pictorial Field-Book of the War of 1812*. New York: Harper & Brothers, Publishing, 1869.

Machar, Agnes Maule. *The Story of Old Kingston*. Toronto: The Musson Book Co., 1908.

Mackey, Frank. *Steamboat Connection: Montreal to Upper Canada, 1816-1843*. Montreal & Kingston: McGill-Queen's University Press, 2000.

MacLeod, Peter D. *The Canadian Iroquois in the Seven Year's War*. Toronto: Dundurn Press, 1996.

Malcomson, Robert. *Lord of the Lakes: The Naval War on Lake Ontario 1812-1814*. Toronto: Robin Brass Studio, 1998.

Mathews, Hazel C. *Frontier Spies: The British Secret Service, Northern Department during the Revolutionary War*. Fort Myers, Florida: Ace Press, Inc., 1971.

Moore, Christopher. *The Loyalists: Revolution, Exile, Settlement*. Toronto: McClelland & Stewart Inc, 1984 (Christopher Moore Editorial Ltd, 1994).

Morris, John D. *Sword of the Border: Major General Jacob Jennings Brown 1775-1828*. Kent, Ohio: The Kent State University Press, 2000.

Pringle, Jacob Farrand. *The Old Eastern District: Its Settlement and Early Progress*. Cornwall: S.I.., 1890.

Quimby, Robert S. *The U.S. Army in the War of 1812: An Operational and Command Study*. 2 Vols. East Lansing, Michigan: Michigan State University Press, 1997.

Reilly, Robin. *The British at the Gates: The New Orleans Campaign in the War of 1812*. Toronto: Robin Brass Studio, 2002 (first published by G.P Putnam's in 1974).

Sellar, Robert. *The U.S. Campaign of 1813 to Capture Montreal*. Hungtington, Quebec: Gleaner Officer, 1913.

Sheppard, George. *Plunder, Profit and Paroles: A Social History of the War of 1812 in Upper Canada*. Montreal & Kingston: McGill-Queen's University Press, 1994.

Stanely, George. *The War of 1812: Land Operations*. Canadian War Museum Historical Publication No. 18. Toronto: Macmillian of Canada in collaboration with the National War Museum of Man, National Museum of Canada, 1983.

Thomas, Earle. *Sir John Johnson: Loyalist Baronet*. Toronto: Dundurn, 1986.

Turner, Wesley B. *British Generals in the War of 1812: High Command in the Canadas*. Montreal and Kingston: McGill-Queen's University Press, 1999.

Van Every, Dale. *Ark of the Empire: The American Frontier 1784-1803*. New York: Quill William Morrow, 1963.

Weller, Jac. *Wellington in the Peninsula*. London: Greenhill Books, 1992 (first published by Nicholas Vane in 1967).

Wilder, Patrick. *The Battle of Sackett's Harbor 1813*. Baltimore: The Nautical & Aviation Publishing Company of America, 1994.

Zaslow, Morris ed. and Wesley Turner. *The Defended Border: Upper Canada and the War of 1812*. Toronto: The Macmillian Company of Canada Limited, 1964.

ARTICLES

Bond, Major C.C.J. "The British Base at Carleton Island", *Ontario History*. Vol. LII No. March 1960, Willowdale: Ontario Historical Society, 1960.

Cruikshank, Ernest A. 'A Study of Disaffection in Upper Canada in 1812-15', *The Defended Border: Upper Canada and the War of 1812* (Morris Zaslow ed.). Toronto: The Macmillian Company of Canada Limited, 1964 (first appeared in the 'Transactions' of the Royal Society of Canada, series three, section 2, 1912).

Malcomson, Robert. "War on Lake Ontario: A Costly Victory at Oswego, 1814", *The Beaver*. Vol. 75:2 April/May 1995. Winnipeg: Canada's National Historical Society, 1995.

Phifer, Mike. "Last Stand at Moraviantown", *Blackpowder Annual 2002*. Union City, Tennessee: Pioneer Press, 2002.

Rawlyk, George A. "Loyalist Military Settlements in Upper Canada". *The Loyal Americans: The Military Role of the Loyalist Provincial Corps and Their Settlements in British North America, 1775-1784*. Ottawa: National Museum of Canada, 1983.

Senior, Elinor Kyte. "The Loyalists in Cornwall 1784-1984," *None was ever better . . . "The Loyalist Settlement of Ontario": Proceedings of the Annual Meeting of the Ontario Historical Society Cornwall, June 1984*. Stormont, Dundas and Glengarry Historical Society, July 1984.

Smith, P.G. "Birth of the Canadian Army", *Military History*. Vol. 20 No. 4. Leesburg, Va.: Primedia Inc, October 2003.

Stacey, C.P. C.P. 'The Defence of Upper Canada, 1812', *The Defended Border: Upper Canada and the War of 1812* (Morris Zaslow ed). Toronto: The Macmillian Company of Canada Limited, 1964 (taken from 'Introduction to the Study of Military History for Canadian Students' 1960).

Way, Ronald. "The Day of Crysler's Farm", *The Defended Border: Upper Canada and the War of 1812* (Morris Zaslow ed.). Toronto: The Macmillian Company of Canada Limited, 1964 (first appeared in 'Canadian Geographical Journal' Vol 62, June 1962).

Weekes, William M. 'The War of 1812: Civil Authority and Martial Law in Upper Canada', *The Defended Border: Upper Canada and the War of 1812* (Morris Zaslow ed.). Toronto: The Macmillian Company of Canada Limited, 1964 (first appeared in 'Ontario History' Vol. 48 Autumn 1956).

Winston-Clare, C. "A Shipbuilder's War", *The Defended Border: Upper Canada and the War of 1812* (Morris Zaslow ed.). Toronto: The Macmillian Company of Canada Limited, 1964 (first appeared in 'The Mariner's Mirror', Vol. 29, 1943).

INTERNET SOURCES

Buckner, Philip. "Sir John Harvey", *Dictionary of Canadian Biography*. www.biographi.ca.

Christie, Carl. "Joseph Wanton Morrison", *Dictionary of Canadian Biography*. www.biographi.ca.

Fitzpatrick, D.E. "William Gilkison", *Dictionary of Canadian Biography*. www.biographi.ca.

Grodizinski, John R. "Command Structure and Appointments in Upper Canada, 1812-1814." *The War of 1812 Magazine* Issue 1: January 2006, www.napolean-series.org.

Henderson, Robert, ed. "Soldier's Families Under Fire: Ambush at Toussaint Island 1812", *The Discriminating General: The War of 1812 Website*. www.militaryheritage.com/ambush.htm.

Johnson, J.K. "William Johnston", *Dictionary of Canadian Biography*. www.biographi.ca.

Lynde, Adam Norman. "The War from the Saddle: The Diary of Lieutenant John Lang, 19th Light Dragoons", *The Discriminating General: The War of 1812 Website*. www.militaryheritage.ca/lang.htm.

Lynde, Adam Norman. "The War from the Saddle: The Diary of Lieutenant John Lang, 19th Light Dragoons. Part Two", *The Discriminating General: The War of 1812 Website*. www.militaryheritage.ca/lang2.htm.

Rawlyk, George and Janice Potter, "Richard Cartwright", *Dictionary of Canadian Biography*. www.biographi.ca.

Shepard, C.J. "John Crysler", *Dictionary of Canadian Biography*. www.biographi.ca.

Shepard, C.J. "Richard Duncan Fraser", *Dictionary of Canadian Biography*. www.biographi.ca.

Stanely, George F.G. *Conflicts and Social Notes, 1000 Islands: The War of 1812-1814, The Patriot War, 1837-1838*. Parks Canada, 1976, http://members.tripod.com/_Oliver_Kilian/1000islands/IsIn7-Wars/wars.htm.

INDEX

Adams, Andrew, 59.
Adams, Samuel, 108.
Anderson, Charles, 103.
Anderson, Joseph, 35.
Appling, David, 126.
Armstrong, John, 63, 64, 77, 78, 79, 80, 81, 82, 83, 86, 89, 92, 93, 111, 115.
Askin, John, 17.
Aspinwall, Thomas, 66, 67, 70, 71.
Astor, John Jacob, 18.
Ault, Michael, 40, 41.

Backus, Electus, 65, 66, 69, 70.
Baird, Lieutenant, 54.
Barnes, George, 104, 105.
Barnet, George, 110.
Bathurst Lord, 65, 113.
Battersby, Francis, 31.
Baynes, Edward, 31, 32, 44, 65, 67, 69, 70, 71, 85, 109.
Bebe, Lieutenant, 27.
Benedict, T.B., 38, 50.
Boyd, John, 81, 82, 96, 99, 103, 104, 106, 110.
Brock, Isaac, 29, 30, 48.
Brown Jacob, 25, 35, 36, 37, 39, 43, 57, 58, 66, 67, 68, 69, 71, 79, 80, 81, 82, 84, 91, 93, 95, 96, 99, 100, 102, 107, 110, 111, 115, 126, 134.
Brouse, Jacob, 95.
Brown, Samuel, 71.
Bruce, Peggy ,44.
Bruyeres, Ralph Henry, 49, 50.

Burr, Aaron, 77, 78.
Butler, John, 17.

Campbell, Lieutenant, 127.
Carly, Major, 51.
Carleton, Guy (Lord Dorchester), 12, 14, 15, 19, 31.
Cartwright, Richard, 17, 20, 26, 27, 31, 44, 86.
Casey, Samuel, 86.
Chauncey, Isaac, 47, 58, 64, 79, 81, 82, 84, 92, 93, 122, 126, 128.
Chauncey, Wolcott, 70, 71.
Church, D.W., 40, 43, 51, 54.
Clark, Duncan, 94.
Clark, Isaac, 60.
Claus, Daniel, 108.
Cochrane, Captain, 100.
Cockburn, Major, 85, 112.
Coles, Isaac, 104.
Collier, Edward, 123.
Comins, James, 53.
Conkey, Joshua, 54.
Cook, George, 108.
Covington, Leonard, 82, 96, 103, 104, 105.
Craig, Henry Knox, 105, 106.
Craig, James, 26.
Crawford, William, 11, 12.
Cross, Lieutenant, 26.
Crysler, John, 98, 101, 131.

Dearborn, Henry, 36, 40, 54, 58, 63, 64, 77.
Deserontyon, John, 12.

De Gaugreben, Frederick, 49, 53, 55, 74, 128, 129.
De Montigny, Louvigny, 44, 45.
Dennis, James, 85, 100.
Denyke, Andrew, 27.
De Rottenberg, Francis, 52, 53, 73, 86, 97, 116, 117.
De Salaberry, Charles -Michel, 87, 89.
De Watteville, Louis, 88.
Dimock, Major, 75, 76.
Dixon, Captain, 75.
Dodge, Richard, 43.
Drummond, Gordon, 116, 117, 122, 123, 124, 125.
Drummond, William, 66, 68, 69, 70.
Drury, John, 70, 71.
Dulmage, Captain, 41.
Dunlap, William, 33, 44, 107, 114.
Durham, Lord, 132.

Earl, Hugh, 30.
Elliot, Matthew, 23.
Eustace, Captain, 55, 56.
Eustis, Abram, 95.
Eustis, William, 36.

Fawcett, Lieutenant, 76.
Finlay, John, 60.
Fischer, Victor, 124.
FitzGibbons, James, 40.
Fitzpatrick, William, 94.
Ford, Judge, 114.
Ford, Nathan, 18, 19, 20.
Forsyth, Benjamin, 35, 42, 43, 49, 50, 51, 52, 54, 55, 56, 57, 95, 96, 115, 134.
Fraser, Richard Duncan, 41, 56, 59, 94, 98, 118, 132.
Fraser, Thomas, 59, 118, 127, 128.
Fraser, William, 34.
Freer, Noah, 113.
French, Gershom, 9.
Frend, Richard, 75, 76.
Fuller, Andrew, 51.

Gilkson, Willam, 18, 21, 44, 77, 111, 117, 118.
Gore, Francis, 26, 27, 29, 31.
Gourlay, Robert, 132.
Grant, Lieutenant, 52.
Grass, Michael, 12.
Gray, Andrew, 45, 46, 47, 65.
Gray, William, 44.
Green, John, 115.
Gregory, Francis, 107.
Griffin, Captain, 40.

Haldimand, Frederic, 9, 12, 13, 14.
Hamilton, Robert, 17.
Hampton, Wade, 78, 79, 80, 83, 85, 87, 88, 89, 92, 93, 94, 96, 107.
Harrison, William Henry, 23, 86.
Harvey, John, 97, 104, 105, 106, 109, 110, 111, 133.
Harvey, John (Midshipman), 110.
Hawkesworth, George, 110.
Heriot, Frederick, 61, 103.
Hewett, John, 125.
Hoard, Silivus, 21.
Hoople, Mary Whitmore, 108.
Hubbard, Abner, 37.
Hubbard, Captain, 28, 39.
Hull. William, 31.

Irvine, Henry, 105.
Izard, George, 88, 89, 115.

Jackson, Andrew, 134.
Jackson, Henry, 99.
Jefferson, Thomas, 29.
Jenkins, John, 53, 55, 56, 57.
Jessup, Edward, 9, 18, 74.
Johnson, John, 9, 11, 12, 13.
Johnson. Lieutenant, 50.
Johnston, William, 80, 132.
Jones, Daniel, 118.
Jones, David, 9.
Jones, Durham, 38.
Jones, Jonas, 56.
Jones, Solomon, 37, 118.

Kellog, Captain, 54.

Kerr, John, 56, 112.
King, William, 93.

Landon, Captain, 127.
Lang, John, 74.
Laval, Jacint, 70.
Le Couteur, John, 71.
Lethbridge, Robert, 32, 33, 43.
Lewis, Morgan, 79, 81, 92, 96, 107, 110.
Lorimer, Verne Francis, 19.
Lovell, Dr., 109, 110.
Lowrie, Ensign, 56.
Luckett, Nelson, 85.
Lydle, Captain, 50.
Lyons, Captain, 45.

MacAulay, James, 55.
Macdonell, Alexander, 30, 53.
Macdonell, George, 30, 31, 45, 46, 52, 53, 54, 55, 56, 57, 58, 87, 88, 89, 114, 153.
Mackenzie, H. 26.
Mackenzie, William, Lyon, 132.
Macomb, Alexander, 18.
Macomb, Alexander (Colonel), 82, 95, 96.
MacPherson, Donald, 33.
Martin, John, 75.
Massey, Hart, 25, 27.
McDonnell, Captain, 44, 45.
McIntyre, Amos, 119.
McKay, John, 56.
McLean, Neil, 35, 45, 46, 52, 59.
McMillan, Alex, 88, 90.
McMillian, Alexander, 45, 52.
McNiff, Patrick, 14.
McNitt, Samuel, 42, 68, 69.
McSween, Sgt., 51.
Merkley, George, 89, 90.
Mitchell, George, 123, 125.
Molson, John, 34.
Morrison, Joseph, 97, 98, 99, 101, 103, 104, 105, 106, 109, 112, 114, 125.
Mulcaster, William, 91, 92, 97, 98, 99, 102, 109, 110, 112, 125.

Munroe, John, 41, 95.

Napoleon, 23, 24, 55.
Noon, Captain, 38.

O'Conner, Richard, 124.
Ogden, Samuel, 18, 19, 20.
Osborne, Thomas, 115, 116.

Parish, David, 20, 21, 38, 43, 54, 58, 77, 114, 134, 135.
Parlow, John, 99.
Pearce, Cromwell, 105.
Pearson, Thomas, 43, 44, 52, 53, 60, 74, 77, 85, 90, 94, 104, 105, 106, 117, 118, 134.
Plenderleath, Charles, 97, 105, 106.
Prevost, George, 29, 30, 40, 46, 49, 50, 53, 56, 58, 60, 64, 65, 66, 67, 70, 71, 76, 77, 86, 88, 97, 113, 117, 122, 123, 128.
Popham, Stephen, 126.
Porter, Moses, 82, 96.
Powell, Ensign, 56.
Proctor, Henry, 73.
Purdy, Robert, 88, 89.

Richards, Benjamin, 89, 99.
Ridge, Adjutant, 55.
Ridout, Thomas, 108, 114, 115, 127.
Ripley, Eleazer Wheelock, 103, 104.
Robinson, Commissary-General, 128.
Ross, John, 114, 115.
Rosseel, Joseph, 21, 38, 58,.

Sacket, Augustus, 25, 26.
Scott, Hercules, 100, 112, 113.
Scott, John, 75.
Seely, Joseph, 119.
Shaver, Lieutenant, 112.
Sheaffe, Roger Hale, 48, 63, 64, 73, 88.
Sheek, David, 109.
Sherwood, Justus, 9.

Sherwood, Levius, 59.
Sherwood, Reuben, 51, 52, 101, 111, 112, 132.
Simcoe, John Graves, 16, 19, 31.
Skinner, Captain, 90.
Smith, Arnold, 50.
Snyder, Ensign, 108.
Spafford, Hiram, 94, 118, 132.
Spilsbury, Francis, 91, 126.
Stacey, Samuel, 64.
Stone, Joel, 42, 49, 118, 119.
Stone, Mrs., 42.
Swartout, Robert, 79, 82, 96, 103, 104.
Swift, Joseph, 103, 105.

Tecumseh, 23, 24.
Tenskwatawa, 23, 24.
Tilden, Captain, 45.
Trowbridge, Amasa, 109.
Twiss, William, 11.

Upham, Timothy, 106.

Van Alstyne, Peter, 12.
Van Rensselaer, Solomon, 38.
Viger, Jacques, 62, 63, 68.
Vincent, John, 43, 53, 60, 64, 65, 73, 86, 97.

Yeo, James Lucas, 64, 65, 68, 76, 81, 83, 86, 92, 93, 110, 121, 122, 123, 124, 125, 126.

Wager, Jacob, 99.
Washington, George, 77.
Wayne, Anthony, 82.
Wellesley, Arthur (Duke of Wellington), 23, 129.
Wells, H.W., 39, 50.
Wilkinson, James, 77, 78, 79, 80, 81, 82, 83, 84, 85, 86, 92, 93, 94, 95, 96, 97, 98, 99, 100, 102, 103, 107, 110, 111, 115, 118, 119, 131, 134.
Woodford, John, 104, 106.

Woolsey, Melanchton, 28, 36, 39, 123, 126.

York, Joseph, 43, 54.
York, Mrs. 57.
Young, Colonel, 69.
Young, Guilford Dudley, 44.

www.ingramcontent.com/pod-product-compliance
Lightning Source LLC
Chambersburg PA
CBHW050638160426
43194CB00010B/1718